# THE NEW NOVELLO PART-SONG BOOK

Forty-four British part-songs for mixed voices from Purcell to the present day.

***Editor: Robert Walker.***



NOVELLO
London

NOV 072472

*Cover: "A Village Choir"*
*by Thomas Webster.*
*Reproduced by kind permission of the V&A Picture Library, London.*

*Cover design: Michael Bell Design.*

*Music setting by Stave Origination.*

*ISBN 0-85360-895-4*


*Published in Great Britain by Novello Publishing Limited.*

*Head office:*
*14/15 Berners Street,*
*London W1T 3LJ*

*Tel +44 (0)20 7434 0066*
*Fax +44 (0)20 7287 6329*

*Sales and Hire:*
*Music Sales Distribution Centre,*
*Newmarket Road,*
*Bury St Edmunds,*
*Suffolk IP33 3YB*

*Tel +44 (0)1284 702600*
*Fax +44 (0)1284 768301*

*e-mail music@musicsales.co.uk*



*Printed in Great Britain.*

# Contents

# Introduction

'In the present age a knowledge and love of Music are increasing so much amongst us, that England appears to be returning to her condition near three centuries since, when every social meeting was cheered by the practised skill of its members, and when a gentleman was held to be but imperfectly educated who could not take his part "at sight" in a madrigal.' Thus Edwin George Monk begins his prospectus to *Novello's Part-Song Book*, a monthly magazine ('priced one shilling') first issued on 15th March 1850 to feed what was fast becoming an insatiable appetite for amateur choral music. His rosy view of Elizabethan education is matched only by our own enchanted view of Victorian amateur music making. Have television and compact discs rendered us as passive and recumbent as we like to believe? Were our nineteenth century forebears so much better at these things than we are? I think not. All over Europe, North America and Australasia, there are groups large and small of amateur singers convening in meeting rooms, church halls or members' homes. Under the guidance of talented choral directors, they are making music with as much skill, dedication and delight as ever their antecedents did. This book is for them.

Thanks to the industry of the founders of Novello and Company the archive now holds more than three thousand part-songs. I have examined them all, and others besides. To choose less than fifty out of this wealth of material was a hard, if delightful task, and my thanks go to Tony Orchover and Rob Norman in assisting me in my scrutiny of the highways and byways of the Novello archive. Three principles I kept in mind in selecting those suitable for inclusion: the music must be good, the text should not be embarrassing and, above all, the part-songs should be practical, attractive and rewarding for amateurs to sing. Some of the early nineteenth century part-songs are not now to our musical or literary taste; others, like Alec Rowley's *Frisco City's Grand and Gay* don't have quite the same connotations now as they had when they were written. I regret, too, that so few part-songs written in the last twenty years were suitable for inclusion.

Some part-songs will already be well-known to singers; but no compilation of any value could omit Stanford's *Blue Bird* or Pearsall's *Lay a Garland*. Others less celebrated will, I hope, prove to be a delightful surprise; and Alan Rawsthorne's *Weep You No More* is published for the first time. Some are relatively easy, others offer choirs a challenge. None is without merit, and all deserve a second or third glance. I have not included madrigals because they are not strictly part-songs; more comprehensive and scholarly collections of madrigals may be found elsewhere. In keeping with its sister publication, *The New Novello Anthem Book*, there are notes on each part-song, its composer and some hints on performance.

All infelicities, omissions and imperfections in this collection fall, of course, to me. I acknowledge with gratitude the help and encouragement given to me by Leslie East, formerly Publishing Director at Novello who also kindly allowed me to use the Rawsthorne manuscript in his possession; and Stephen Meakins, founder and conductor of the Laurence Lloyd Singers in whose company I first discovered the inestimable pleasure of singing part-songs more than thirty years ago.

Robert Walker, Karangasem, Bali 1999

**Robert Walker** wrote his first unaccompanied choral work at the age of 16. It was an arrangement of Rolf Harris's *Tie Me Kangaroo Down, Sport*, and an act of flagrant copyright piracy from which the publishing world is still reeling. He was singing in three choirs at the time, because the alto standing next to him caught his eye. He was tragically spurned, which accounts for the revengeful, tortuous difficulty of all subsequent alto parts in his choral music, and the anguished nature of all his music. Whilst conducting the Great St. Mary's Singers from the tower of the Cambridge church on May Day morning 1967 (*fa-la-la*), he made a dramatic gesture and nearly fell into the traffic below. Fortunately he remained sufficiently unscathed later to found the Jesus Singers in Cambridge, the Grimsby Bach Choir in Lincolnshire (for whom he wrote *Five Summer Madrigals*) and the Sutton and Bignor Singers in Sussex – and he still bears the scars. In 1992 he removed himself from all temptation and went to live on the island of Bali where he composes, plays gamelan and where there are no choirs.

# *Notes on the Part-Songs by Robert Walker*

**1. The Blue Bird · Charles Villiers Stanford** (1852-1924)
From early childhood Stanford was exposed to the amateur music-making of a group of intellectuals – doctors, judges, clerics – who frequented his parents' Dublin home. While still an undergraduate he conducted the Cambridge Amateur Vocal Guild. Curiously, despite his prodigious output, he came late to writing part-songs; the first dates from his fortieth year. Although Stanford marked the top line of *The Blue Bird* to be sung by all the sopranos, it is common practice and very effective to assign this to a soprano solo; the other sopranos taking the first alto part. I have arranged the staves to facilitate this. The phrased staccatos should be taken very deliberately and the whole work sung with an air of simplicity. *The Blue Bird* works so well because it is so simple.

**2. Breathe Soft, Ye Winds · William Paxton** (1737-1781)
Paxton was a cellist and a Roman Catholic, so on both counts he was impeded from entering the then very Anglican world of choral music. Nevertheless his glees won many plaudits, and he was awarded two Catch Club prizes. Some scholars think this glee (originally a trio) may have been written by his brother Stephen. The form clearly derives from the minuet (including the Haydnesque hemiola at the cadences), so it requires a minuet-like speed and a dancing rhythm.

**3. Bring Us in Good Ale · Gustav Holst** (1874-1934)
Holst's entry into the musical pantheon was a hesitant one. He failed three times to gain a scholarship at London's Royal College of Music. He supported himself by playing trombone on Brighton Pier in the summer holidays, and in pantomimes in London theatres during the Christmas break. Whilst still a student he conducted the Hammersmith Socialist Choir which met at the house of the designer, poet and architect William Morris. When he married Isobel Harrison in 1901 his only income was from two published part-songs and his trombone. This jolly piece was written in 1916 – about the same time he was working on *The Planets*. To bring this off, a cracking pace, precise rhythm and, above all, panache are required.

**4. Cargoes · Henry Balfour Gardiner** (1877-1950)
A splendid example of an English eccentric, Balfour Gardiner's greatest achievement was to use his substantial private income to support his less fortunate contemporaries, particularly Holst (qv), Grainger and Delius – whose house in France he purchased to enable the ailing Delius to see out the rest of his declining life there. Balfour Gardiner stopped composing in 1925 to begin pioneering, ecological work in forestry at his Dorset estate. *Cargoes* was written in 1912. Be alert to the dotted rhythms: when Gardiner intends a triplet he writes one. Begin the *Allegro* fairly cautiously; leave yourself plenty of room to get faster. The recommendation to use a quartet in the first verse is the composer's, but unless the soloists are very good, a semi-chorus is probably better.

**5. Celandine · Robert Walker** (b. 1946)
This is the last of six interlinked songs I wrote for The Scholars in 1973. The compositional idea behind it was to bring the technique of Anglican psalm-singing into the secular world of the part-song. By keeping the sense of the words foremost in your mind as you chant them, the natural stresses of speech will be your guide to the variable rhythms. Take the wide leaps easily and smoothly, with no sense of urgency. The empty bar at the end is quite deliberate.

**6. Come Away, Death · George Alexander Macfarren** (1813-97)
When he was just 17, Macfarren conducted his 1st Symphony at a Royal Academy of Music concert in London. Seven years later he was made a professor of that institution. In the meantime he had already founded the Society of British Musicians in 1834 and, ten years later, established the Handel Society. By this time he was almost totally blind, but composed, taught and conducted prolifically all his long life. If, like many, your choir is short of tenors, with a little ingenuity the second tenor part can be assigned to baritones, except at bars 50-55 where altos might take over the first tenor part. A carefully planned breathing scheme is required here, and due observance of rests is important.

**7. Come Let Us Join the Roundelay · William Beale** (1784-1854)
After his voice broke and his services were no longer required as a chorister at Westminster Abbey, Beale signed up as a midshipman. Aged 36, he became the organist of Trinity College, Cambridge but only lasted a year. He turned up next as organist of Wandsworth Parish Church, London and later at St. John's, Clapham Rise. His only claims to fame are this self-styled 'madrigal' and a prize awarded in 1840 by the Adelphi Glee Club. This part-song was originally for male voices but is more generally known in this SATB version. Think two-in-a-bar and treat the rhythms lightly, as befits a 'madrigal'.

**8. Come Live with Me · W. Sterndale Bennett** (1816-75)
Mendelssohn, who invited him to Germany after

hearing him play his own first Piano Concerto, knew this 17 year old boy only as 'William Bennett'. 'Sterndale' was added by his upwardly mobile descendants subsequent to his high reputation and knighthood. Schumann, too, became particularly attached to the young Mr. Bennett as soon as they met, and sang his praises in *Neue Zeitschrift für Musik* as early as 1837. He was thought to be the Great White Hope of British music but, like Mendelssohn – whom he most admired – Bennett's best work was written in his teens and early twenties. The exigencies of teaching and playing wore him down. *Come Live With Me* was written in 1846. The metronome mark is Bennett's and, if observed, ensures this part-song sings itself.

**9. Cupid and Rosalind · Charles Villiers Stanford**
As a choral scholar of Queen's College, Cambridge, Stanford was naturally drawn to choral music. This part-song was written around 1894 and is part of a huge series to Elizabethan texts which Stanford embarked upon at this time. The rocking vocal lines work wonderfully well if they are delicately and accurately sung. Moderation is required in those passages marked staccato; if overdone, they might sound frivolous.

**10. Echoes · Arthur Sullivan** (1842-1900)
By accepting and issuing the song *O Israel*, Novello became the first publisher of Arthur Sullivan. The composer was just 13 years old. He learned his craft from Sterndale Bennett (qv) at the Royal Academy of Music. It is unsurprising therefore to catch the strong influence of Mendelssohn in all his works. He was a social animal and reckoned the Duke of Edinburgh (Queen Victoria's favourite son) as a close friend. The bizarre peculiarity of this delightful part-song is the long hiatus which crops up from time to time between phrases and verses. It's best to make a virtue of it – even perhaps slightly over-stretching the gap – leaving the audience with a sense of anticipation.

**11. Evening Has Lost Her Throne · Granville Bantock** (1868-1946)
When Bantock succeeded Elgar (qv) as Professor of Music at Birmingham University, he investigated and became an early authority on Elizabethan music; but there is little evidence of that here. If Wagner had written part-songs, this might have been one of them. The tempo needs to be very broad and flexible in true Wagnerian fashion. Shortly after the *poco tranquillo* the tempo must move on dramatically through the sequences before coming to settle again at bar 19. Resume the *poco tranquillo* tempo at bar 20, only to move on again. *Morendo* is marked at the end, but this should not imply too much of a *rit.*

**12. Fruit Machine · Bryan Kelly** (b. 1934)
After the usual, wholesome path of guidance from Herbert Howells (qv) at the Royal College of Music, Bryan Kelly took the road only slightly less travelled, and studied in Paris with Nadia Boulanger. Like others – mostly Americans – before him (Ned Rorem and Paul Bowles come to mind), his time in France gave his music a frothy sense of vitality and a disposition for jokes. Like all good, spontaneous comedy, the jokes come off only if their execution is meticulously rehearsed down to the last raised eyebrow. Kelly has helped by being meticulous himself with articulation and dynamic markings. Projecting the lyrics across to your audience is imperative here. Bryan Kelly has collaborated many times with the poet John Fuller and the words are by no means secondary to the music.

**13. Go, Lovely Rose · Eric Thiman** (1900-75)
Thiman was largely self-taught, which explains the academicism pervading much of his output; it is sometimes dull, but never slovenly. Occasionally, however, he produced a carefully wrought gem, and this is one of them. Thiman's whole world was amateur music making: adjudicator at competitive festivals, examiner for the Associated Board and external examiner to university faculties. Thus his music is finely written for amateur singers. This simple but effective part-song was written when the composer was 26. It is tempting to slow down at the end of each verse, but Thiman has written in a *rit.* with the 3/2 bar before the cadence. Keep it moving.

**14. Inheritance · Herbert Howells** (1892-1983)
There are few English composers whose style is as immediately recognisable as that of Herbert Howells. *Inheritance* is the secular twin of his more famous, later motet, *Take Him, Earth, for Cherishing* (1964). It forms part of the collection of part-songs, given the overall title of *A Garland for the Queen*, commissioned from many leading British composers for the coronation of Queen Elizabeth II in 1953. Make full use of Howells's injunction *sempre un poco rubato*; the metronome marking is slow and the long melismas need to move on a bit. The modern jazz harmonies, reminiscent of Earl Hines, require very precise intonation, especially at the enharmonic cadences. Avoid any sense of religiosity. Howells once said 'I am not a religious man any more than Ralph [Vaughan Williams] was.'

**15. In These Delightful, Pleasant Groves · Henry Purcell** (1659-95)
In the vast output of Purcell's music for voices, very few examples exist of glees in four voices. Most, like the catches, are in three parts or require an independent accompaniment. This glee is in fact a chorus from the masque *The Libertine* and may properly include a string or thorough-bass accompaniment. I have deliberately left it uncluttered as it appears in Ian Spinks's edition in Purcell Society Volume 20. Make something special of those extraordinary arrests of rhythm in the first section. A brisk tempo and *leggiero* style of singing, especially in the runs on the word 'laugh', are required.

**16. In This Hour of Softened Splendour · Ciro Pinsuti** (1829-88)
The Italian Pinsuti was a child prodigy, making his debut as a pianist in his home town of Sinalunga at the age of 9. Two years later he was brought to London to study composition – an unusual reversal of the normal procedure then in vogue. He settled in London in 1848 where he coached opera singers; but he maintained links with Italy. Three of his operas were produced in Bologna, Milan and Venice. It is effective to stagger the breathing during the long melisma and run straight into the reprise of '*In this hour*' without a break. The dotted rhythms need careful timing to avoid any sense of triplets.

**17. Invocation to Sleep · Julius Benedict** (1804-85)
Sir Julius (sometimes 'Jules') Benedict was born in Stuttgart and became first a pupil then a close friend of Weber. He was a prolific composer and an inexhaustible champion of all causes in music. He, like Pinsuti, is an example of that company of continental composers who transmigrated to a better life in England, 'das Land ohne Musik' as the received opinion had it. Six of his part-songs (of which this is one) formed the very first volume of the original Novello Part-Song Book. At first glance this seems a gently flowing, uneventful little piece, but the metronome mark belies this. It requires considerable stamina to get through the phrases of what is actually rather a dark work.

**18. John Cook · Thea Musgrave** (b. 1928)
A Scot by birth, Thea Musgrave has lived since 1972 in the United States. At a time when it was uncommon for women to join the ranks of professional composers, she carved a reputation for herself which has grown enormously over the years. All her music possesses a keen sense of drama, and her operas are perhaps her major achievement. The drama in *John Cook* is all in the semitones, so attention to tuning these small shifts is important. After bar 53, the *sforzandos* on 'down' must drop instantly to a *piano* sufficient to allow the very low basses to come through.

**19. Lay a Garland · Robert Pearsall** (1795-1856)
Robert Lucas Pearsall died in Switzerland. On medical advice after a stroke at the age of 30, he had lived most of his life in the cleaner air of 'abroad'. Pearsall was perhaps the earliest British example of a student of ancient music, and it was his indefatigable efforts which helped to establish our abiding love for madrigals. He was an original member of the Bristol Madrigal Society (1837) where many of his own compositions – often in the 'ancient' style – were performed. He remained almost unknown elsewhere. *Lay a Garland* is one of the earliest and most beautiful part-songs in the repertoire. The more *maestoso* the better for this elegy to a jilted maiden. Especially if yours is a large choir, the 'harmonium' effect of staggered breathing can add spine-shivering power as the layers of sound build and crunch on the suspensions.

**20. The Long Day Closes · Arthur Sullivan**
Sullivan loved to travel widely with friends. Most of his songs and part-songs were written for money to sustain his high life; so, when fame and fortune as the musical half of the comic opera team finally came his way, he stopped writing them and took up the more lucrative pastime of gambling. Sullivan's cautionary injunction *non troppo largo* should be heeded. If taken too slowly this part-song grinds to a halt at the ends of the verses. The loud, unison moment at bar 27ff can be embarrassing unless handled carefully and simply; best not to make a crisis out of a drama. Sullivan has written in the *rit.* at the end, so keep the pulse constant.

**21. Madrigal · Richard Rodney Bennett** (b. 1936)
Bennett, who studied with Boulez, has shown an extraordinary versatility and range in his compositions; sometimes cerebrally dodecaphonic, at others bordering on the sublime. No-one who has heard it can ever forget the waltz from the film version of *Murder on the Orient Express* as the train pulls out of Istanbul. Bennett continues to play jazz in New York night clubs and sing, close-miked, in a husky light baritone, but he still finds time to write vast amounts of music. The constant shifts of rhythm from two groups of three to three groups of two in this *Madrigal* are both its charm and its dilemma. Precision is critical. Take note of the numerous accents which emphasise the cross-rhythms.

**22. The Moon · George Dyson** (1883-1964)
On the proceeds of his Mendelssohn Scholarship young George bummed around Germany and Italy for four years before settling down to become a public school master; an activity which culminated in thirteen years as Director of Music at Winchester College. In 1938 he returned to his old alma mater as Director of the Royal College of Music where he remained until he retired to his beloved Winchester in 1952. Amateur music making was always central to him and he spent a good deal of his efforts promoting it as an adjudicator at competitive festivals and conductor of choral societies and amateur orchestras. The Three Choirs Festival was his home territory, where many of his oratorios were premiered. You will notice there is not a single rest in *The Moon* apart from the obvious ones at bar 43 (where, although Dyson indicates nothing, it is safe to assume the pulse remains the same). Dyson intends a seamless thread of fast shifting harmonies ebbing and flowing. Aim for very sustained vocal lines uninterrupted by too many breaths.

**23. Music,When Soft Voices Die · Geoffrey Bush** (1920-98)
Perhaps because he was a chorister at Salisbury Cathedral, Geoffrey Bush's most characteristic music is for voices: stage-works, choral pieces and solo songs.

With a natural affinity for a wide range of texts (from Chaucer to Stevie Smith via Jonson, Wilde and Virginia Woolf) – his music always serves to embellish and illuminate the given word. The often occurring quaver rest and two semiquavers determine the slow speed of this part-song; 'when soft' (*et al.*) is difficult not to gabble and very tempting to turn into a triplet. The canonical tenors' dynamics in the first verse are marked up a notch.

**24. My Delight and Thy Delight · C. Hubert H. Parry** (1848-1918)
The aristocratic Parry gained his MusB degree while he was still a schoolboy at Eton under the aegis of George Elvey (qv). After leaving Oxford he worked for Lloyd's Register of Shipping. Radical in politics, ethics and aesthetics, he influenced a whole generation of musicians and gained all the highest positions and accolades the British musical establishment could bestow. His book, *The Art of Music* written in 1892, attempted to apply Darwinian theories of evolution to music history. Not everyone admired him: the pedagogue R.O. Morris called Parry's series of choral works 'able failures'. Parry was a rare bird in the musical scene of late Victorian England: he was never a professional organist. His word setting is always exemplary, and in *My Delight...* he very cleverly juxtaposes phrases beginning on the first beat with anacruses in others. Extended phrase lengths and syncopations move the music forward towards each climax.

**25. My Soul Would Drink Those Echoes · Alexander Mackenzie** (1847-1935)
To support himself as a student at the Royal Academy of Music the Edinburgh-born Mackenzie played violin in London theatre orchestras. He was only 15 years old. At 18 he returned to Edinburgh where he organised concerts of contemporary music. It was Mackenzie who shocked Scottish ears with Schumann's Piano Quartet and Quintet. At 32 he left Scotland and moved to Florence to devote himself to composition. But in 1885, he was asked to conduct the Novello Oratorio Concerts, so returned to settle in London. Under his baton, major contemporary oratorios by many composers, including Dvorák and Liszt, were heard for the first time. Three years later, he succeeded Sir George Macfarren (qv) as Principal of the R.A.M. For good or ill, his was the guiding light by which the Associated Board of the Royal Schools of Music was founded. Treat this part-song like an operatic chorus full of tense pauses, highlighted dynamics and dramatic changes of tempo. Don't be cautious with the tempo markings, but aim for a Byronic, extravagant abandon.

**26. O Sing unto My Roundelay · Samuel Wesley** (1766-1837)
Sam was the nephew of the founder of Methodism and, in 1774, Dr. Boyce visited the Wesley household in Bristol to hear for himself 'the English Mozart'. But Charles Wesley had more scruples than Leopold Mozart and discouraged his 12 year old son, already the composer of the oratorio *Ruth,* from too much musical activity in favour of a thorough, classical eduction. Later Sam himself was to comment: 'The musical "trade" is a trivial and degrading business to any man of spirit or of any abilities.' Uncle John was happy to concur. Sam withdrew more and more from the public gaze to live a life of study (especially in his passion for Bach) and composition. His small circle of Bach-loving friends ('The Bach Junta' he called them) included Vincent Novello, who organised a subscription in 1830 to rescue Sam from penury. Mann's editorial markings in *O Sing unto My Roundelay* perhaps over-compensate for Wesley's deficiency, and you are free to ignore them. But Mann does correct a few ungrammatical *faux pas* which the 'English Mozart' and student of Bach seems to have missed.

**27. Orpheus, with His Lute · George Macfarren**
Apparently, Macfarren was never slow in offering opinions. His most notable quote is: 'Beethoven is sometimes weak. Mozart never.' But others were equally dismissive of him. Wagner wrote in a letter: 'Mr. Macfarrine (*sic.*) [is] a pompous and unruly Scotsman.' He was in fact English; the son of a London dancing master. To make some sense of this very awkward Shakespeare text it is essential not to take a breath after 'freeze', and 'sea' (bar 32) even though Macfarren's phrasing suggests otherwise. The pulse should be maintained briskly or the coda will grind to a halt.

**28. The Prince of Sleep · Edward Elgar** (1857-1934)
Elgar has been heavily researched, yet few studies mention his part-songs in any detail. He wrote many, and they display all the originality, variety and profound musicianship to be found in his larger works. This comparatively late work (1925) requires some discerning phrase work and sustained breath control. Take the *più mosso* section with a swing.

**29. Proud Songsters · John McCabe** (b. 1939)
A man of many parts, John McCabe is a composer in most genres including television, a pianist and cricket lover. His ballet *Edward II* has created a sensation wherever it has been performed. McCabe marks this tribute to the Mancunian choral director Stephen Wilkinson *deciso*. Take him at his word with some vigour, fanfare and panache. The dynamics play an important part in keeping up the momentum. Be aware of pronunciation when the voices are at the top of their registers.

**30. A Shepherd's Carol · Benjamin Britten** (1913-76)
Despite its appearance in carol books, I am yet to be convinced this cheery little work has anything whatever to do with Christmas; so I include it here with no apology. You must make what you will of the Auden verses. I am inclined to think he was characteristically

taking the mickey out of us all. Sung tongue-in-cheek (if that is physically possible...), with large spoonfuls of camp drama, this miniature never fails to delight audiences. Eschew rehearsing the rhythm of the chorus slowly, it only confuses singers even more; they should just 'feel' it. Choose your soloists carefully; their sense of humour is more essential than the quality of their voices. Depending on the acoustics, you might like to place the soloists in different locations.

**31. Sigh No More Ladies · E.J. Moeran** (1894-1950)
Having returned wounded from the First World War, Moeran tried to make a go of being a successful music master at his old school Uppingham. But his heart was elsewhere and he quickly resigned to study composition again with John Ireland. His self-criticism was acute and he spent most of his life in a search of a personal voice for his music. But his contemporaries – Delius, Ireland and especially Peter Warlock (with whom he shared lodgings for a short while) dominated his style and he never quite shrugged off their influence. He died of a heart attack after falling from a pier at Kenmare in Ireland. Take the flowing, erratic rhythms smoothly but steadily, or the phrase ends (especially in the altos) will be swallowed up by the necessary breaths. The *poco accel.* needs to push the music convincingly towards the *poco animato*. The following 'hey nonny' section could sound prissy if not sung lightly and quite fast.

**32. Sleep! The Bird Is in Its Nest · Joseph Barnby** (1836-96)
'Mr. Joseph Barnby's Choir' was founded in 1867 and four years later, with the combined choirs of London's leading churches, gave the first performance in Britain of Bach's *St. Matthew Passion*, an event which had the most profound effect on the English choral tradition. Later, Barnby's choir combined with the Royal Albert Hall Choral Society to become The Royal Choral Society which happily still flourishes. This delightful piece of Victoriana comes off well if you hold back the first two bars of each verse, *accel.* towards the top of the phrase (eg. bar 5) and then relax the tempo again on the way down. Offer a slight *rall.* before the pauses. Experiment with semi-choruses or soloists for different verses.

**33. Softly, Softly Blow Ye Breezes · George Elvey** (1816-93)
Elvey was Samuel Sebastian Wesley's great rival in the back-stabbing world of church music. At the age of just 20, his anthem *Bow Down Thine Ear* defeated Wesley's *The Wilderness* to the Gresham Prize; and at 21 he pipped Wesley to the prestigious post of organist at St. George's Chapel, Windsor. But time has reversed their fortunes and Elvey is now almost forgotten as a composer. The basses in *Softly, Softly...* act as a kind of pizzicato accompaniment to the much smoother upper voices. Don't let this part-song drag, especially at the ends of verses.

**34. Song of Proserpine · Samuel Coleridge-Taylor** (1875-1912)
Can we now imagine the struggles of Samuel Coleridge Taylor? Not only was his father black, but he abandoned the family home and left the infant Samuel to be brought up by his English mother in Croydon and dire straits. At the age of 15, a benefactor sent him to the RCM as a violin student. At 16, his first compositions were published by the ever perspicacious Novello. Coleridge-Taylor is an early, unsung hero of the early black consciousness movement, and was hailed in the U.S.A. as a standard bearer for the cause. For most of his life, he patiently and stoically withstood the rebuffs and indignities heaped on him by English society because of his colour. At one time, he contemplated emigrating to America where players of the New York Philharmonic Orchestra had already dubbed him their 'black Mahler'. Nevertheless, for some reason he stuck it out in Croydon to the end. *Song of Proserpine* is so short, but so dramatic, it makes a marvellous opening number to a concert. Wallow in the harmonies and give the *poco accel.* a lot of gas.

**35. Sweet and Low · Joseph Barnby**
Barnby was an expert choir trainer and insisted on high standards both in vocal production and musical repertoire. He conducted the first performance of *Parsifal* in England only two years after its premiere in Bayreuth. *Sweet and Low* has been treated with a contempt it does not deserve. If sung straight, without exaggerating the dynamics or squeezing *rubatos*, it has a wonderful simplicity, and is particularly effective as an encore.

**36. Sweet Content · John Joubert** (b. 1927)
In 1952, Joubert won the Novello Anthem Competition with *O Lorde, the Maker of Al Thing* and this put his name in the public gaze. At the time he was a lecturer at Hull University, where he remained until 1962. That year he moved to Birmingham where he has lived and composed ever since. *Sweet Content* is quite challenging in the matter of intonation. Voices find it difficult to make a clear distinction between the F sharp in bar 1 and the F natural in bar 2, for instance. The enharmonic changes, too, present a challenge, and occasionally some minor modification to tuning has to be made. The cross-accents of the 'hey nonny' chorus work well if emphasised.

**37. There Is Sweet Music · Edward Elgar**
There can be few composers of Elgar's era who would have dared to write an unaccompanied choral work in eight parts, occasionally in canon, but in two simultaneous keys a semitone apart. It looks alarming at first, but actually makes perfect sense once you get into it. It says much for Elgar that not only did he succeed in this trick, but he produced a work of 'sweet music' into the bargain. The architecture of this piece is problematic; the long *cantilena* lines need careful judgment or the impression as a whole becomes too

sectional. The gentle syncopations should not be stressed heavily but allowed to flow naturally.

**38. There Was an Old Man in a Tree · Mátyás Seiber** (1905-60)
When he was 20, Seiber entered a Wind Sextet for a competition in his native Budapest. He did not win and both Bartók and Kodály, who were on the panel of judges, resigned in protest. After leaving school, Seiber accepted a teaching post in Frankfurt but it didn't suit him. He joined a cruise ship as a cellist and meandered happily around the Americas for a year. He returned to Frankfurt as a lecturer in the theory and practice of jazz. In 1933, when the Nazis took power, he wandered off again; finally coming to rest in Caterham, Surrey, England where he lived for the next quarter century. *There Was an Old Man in a Tree* is typical of Seiber's *mitteleuropäische* style: witty, elegant but with a touch of spite. It needs a jaunty style; there is nothing delicate about this piece. The staccatos, cross-accents and buzzings need to be unsophisticated and sung unaffectedly.

**39. To Daffodils · Harold Darke** (1888-1976)
Three years after becoming organist of St. Michael's Cornhill in the City of London, Harold Darke founded the St. Michael's Singers in 1919. He was still conducting them in 1966. He is best known for a handful of pieces for the church, most notably his transcendent setting of *In the Bleak Midwinter*. A beautifully crafted little piece, *To Daffodils* requires a light touch with careful handling of the dynamics. Don't overdo the hairpins or the *molto ralls*.

**40. To Miss Margery Wentworth · John Joubert**
Commissioned for the Cork International Choral and Folk Dance Festival in 1983, this is a later and less angular work than the other Joubert piece in this compilation. Despite his instruction *con tenerezza*, keep the rhythm strongly two-in-a-bar throughout to prevent it from sagging. Singing chains of fourths and fifths in tune is troublesome; some separate rehearsals might be helpful.

**41. Tune Thy Music to Thy Heart · Walford Davies** (1869-1941)
Walford Davies was the first and only Master of The King's Musick so far to recognise broadcasting as a medium by which popular aesthetics could be conveyed. His talent for enlightening the general public to the byways of music was exemplary. Although an organist, he was also the composer of an Elgarian march which has become the 'anthem' for the Royal Air Force. For four years, from 1919, he was the conductor of the Bach Choir. He had a gratifying ability to turn his hand to good tunes (*Solemn Melody, A.A. Milne Songs,* his superb arrangement of *The Last Post* and so on) and this part-song is amongst them. The opening and subsequent fa-la-las must be taken lightly and fast or the verses will dawdle. Take your cue from the flowing speed of the verses. If you use a baritone soloist, you might like to isolate him to give his voice greater prominence.

**42. Under the Greenwood Tree · Joseph Horovitz** (b. 1926)
To escape Nazi persecution, the Horovitz family fled to England in 1938 when Jo was 12 years old. Later he studied music at Oxford University. Horovitz is best known for his work in film and television, but his contributions to the Hoffnung concerts and his witty pastiche oratorios (especially *Captain Noah and His Floating Zoo* and *Horrortorio*) have endeared him to many. The *Three Choral Songs* from *'As You Like It'* (of which this is No. 2) were commissioned in 1973 by the Exultate Singers. The irregular metre gives this piece an attractive lilt which you should exploit. Take the sudden changes of dynamics at face value.

**43. Weep You No More · Alan Rawsthorne** (1905-71)
Rawsthorne came late to composition after he had tried his hand at dentistry and architecture. Not until he was 33 did he achieve any wide recognition and even then only in the rather rarefied atmosphere of the International Society for Contemporary Music. His chamber music is as finely wrought as that of his two nearest contemporaries: Walton and Tippett. He was publicly scornful of what he called the 'novelty gimmicks' of trendier composers around him, and was shunned by the dedicated followers of fashion as a result. Although marked 'Rather slowly' the long melismatic phrases in *Weep You No More* gain nothing by being too slow. The chromatic shifts need careful tuning to make sense of the rapidly changing and sometimes rather sparse harmonies.

**44. Which Is the Properest Day to Sing? · Thomas Arne** (1710-78)
Because each voice has the limelight somewhere, this part-song makes an admirable opening number to show off the choir. You are free to choose a faster speed than that suggested. The faster the better in drier acoustics; and an *accel.* in the last line finishes it off nicely. The Arnes were upholsterers in London, and Tom's father did sufficiently well to send his son to Eton. It was the Arne siblings (Thomas, Susannah and Richard) who pirated *Acis and Galatea* and produced it at the Haymarket Theatre against Handel's wishes and interests. It forced the almost bankrupt Handel to turn from opera to oratorio – an act from which English music has arguably never recovered.

# 1. THE BLUE BIRD

Text
Mary E. Coleridge

CHARLES VILLIERS STANFORD
(1852 - 1924)

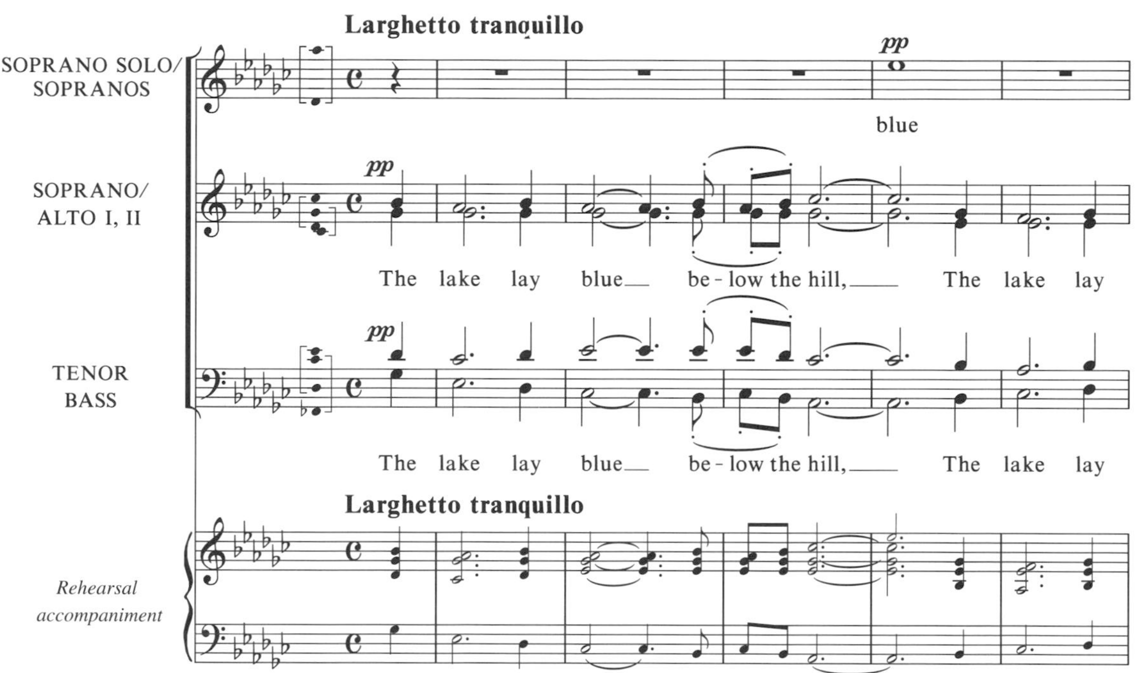

11

looked, there flew A-cross the wa-ters, cold and still, A bird

blue, Cold and still, there

blue, Cold and still, there

15

whose wings were pa-lest blue.

ppp

flew a bird whose wings were pa-lest blue. The

ppp p

flew a bird whose wings were pa-lest blue. The

21

p

blue,

*cresc.*

sky a-bove was blue at last, The sky be-neath me

*cresc.*

sky a-bove was blue at last, The sky be-neath me

27

blue, A mo-ment, ere the bird had

pp

blue in blue, was blue in blue,

pp

blue in blue, was blue in blue,

27

32

mf

passed, It caught his im - - - age, his im-age

mf

blue in blue, It caught, it caught his im - age, his im-age

mf

blue in blue, It caught, it caught his im - age as

32

38

**Più lento**

*quasi niente* ppp

as he flew. blue.

as he flew. The lake lay blue be-low the hill.

he flew. The lake lay blue be-low the hill.

38

**Più lento**

# 2. BREATHE SOFT, YE WINDS

Text
Anon.

WILLIAM PAXTON
(1735 - 1787)

Andante affettuoso
SOPRANO
ALTO
TENOR
BASS
*
p
Breath soft, ye winds, ye wa - ters gent - ly flow,
cresc.
flow'rs a-round
Shield her, ye trees, ye flow'rs a - round
her grow; Breathe soft, ye
pp
Shield her, ye trees, ye flow'rs a - round her grow;
winds, ye wa - ters gent - ly flow,
Shield her, ye trees, ye flow'rs
a-round
a - round her
grow; Ye swains, I beg you pass in si - lence
a-round her
a - round her grow;
p
cresc.

* This arrangement may be sung in D flat if preferred.

20
dim.
cresc.
a-sleep
by, My love in yon - der vale doth lie, my
a - sleep
dim.
cresc.

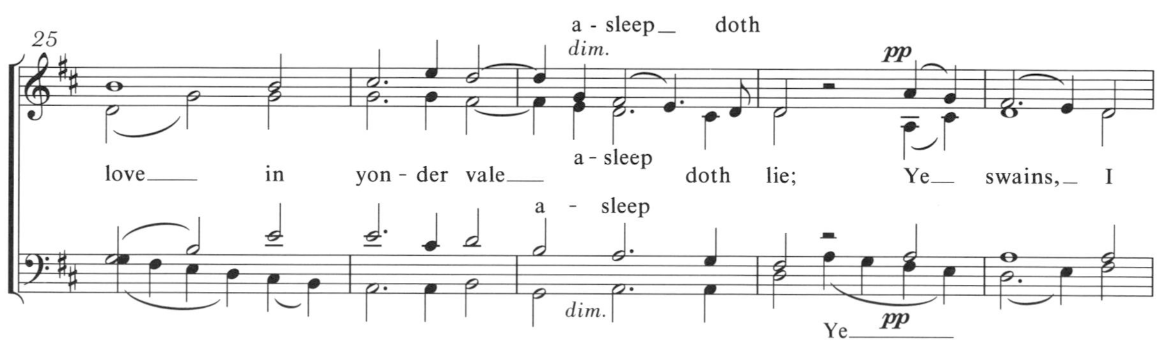
25
a - sleep doth
dim.
pp
love in yon - der vale doth lie; Ye swains, I
a - sleep
a - sleep
dim.
Ye pp

30
cresc.
dim.
yon - der vale
beg you pass in si - lence by, My love in yon - der vale
cresc.
dim.

35
a - sleep doth
cresc.
dim. e rit.
pp
a-sleep doth lie, my love in yon - der vale a-sleep doth lie.
a - sleep
a - sleep
cresc.
div.
pp
dim. e rit.

*To Conrad Noel*

# 3. BRING US IN GOOD ALE

Text
Anon. 16th Century

GUSTAV HOLST
(1874 - 1934)

6
beef for there is ma - ny bones, But bring us in good ale for that goes down at
6
9
mf
Bring us in no ba - con for that is pass - ing fat, But
f
p
onys; And bring us in good ale.
(once)
9
12
bring us in good ale and give us i - nought of that.
(e - nough)
f
And bring us in good ale.
f
Bring us in no
12

mut - ton, for that is of - ten lean; Nor bring us a - ny tripes for they be

*p* Bring us in no eg - gys for there are ma - ny shells, But *cresc.*

*p* Bring us in no eg - gys for there are ma - ny

*p* Bring us in no eg - gys for there are ma - ny

sel - dom clean. *p* But bring us in good ale, But bring us in good ale,

bring us in good ale and bring us no - thing

shells, But *cresc.* bring us in good ale.

shells, But *cresc.* bring us in good ale.

But bring us *cresc.* in good ale, But bring us in good ale.

28
else. But bring us in good
Bring us in no but - - ter for there are ma - ny hairs, Nor
But bring us in good ale.
Bring us in no but - - ter for there are ma - ny hairs, Nor
30
ale.
bring us in no pig's flesh for that will make us bears.
But bring us in good ale.
bring us in no pig's flesh for that will make us bears.
32
Accel.
cresc.
Bring us in good ale, But bring us in good ale, But bring us in good
Bring us in no pud - dings for there in is all God's good; Nor
Bring us in no pud - dings for there in is all God's good; Nor
Bring us in good ale, But bring us in good ale,

34
ale, But bring us in good ale, But bring us in good ale,
bring us in no ve - ni - son for that is not for our blood.
bring us in no ve - ni - son for that is not for our blood.
But bring us in good ale, But bring us in good ale,
34
Presto
36
ff
Bring us in no ca - pon's flesh for that is of - ten dear, Nor
Bring us in no ca - pon's flesh for that is of - ten dear, Nor
Bring us in no ca - pon's flesh for that is of - ten dear, Nor
Bring us in good ale, But bring us in good ale, But bring us in good
36
Presto
38
bring us in no duck's flesh for they slob - ber in the mere,
fff Lento
But bring us in good ale.
bring us in no duck's flesh for they slob - ber in the mere,
fff
But bring us in good ale.
bring us in no duck's flesh for they slob - ber in the mere,
fff
But bring us in good ale.
fff
ale, But bring us in good ale,
But bring us in good ale.
39
Lento

# 4. CARGOES

Text
John Masefield

HENRY BALFOUR GARDINER
(1877 - 1950)

* The First Verse, which begins here, is better sung by a Quartet of Solo Voices.

11
sempre p
ha-ven in sun-ny Pa-les-tine, With a car-go of i-vor-y, and
ha-ven in sun-ny Pa-les-tine, With a car-go of i-vor-y,
ha-ven in sun-ny Pa-les-tine, With a car-go of i-vor-y, and
ha-ven in sun-ny Pa-les-tine, With a car-go of i-vor-y,
17
apes and pea-cocks, San-dal wood, ce-dar wood, and sweet white wine.
apes and pea-cocks, San-dal wood, ce-dar wood, and sweet white wine.
apes and pea-cocks, San-dal wood, ce-dar wood, and sweet white wine.
apes and pea-cocks, San-dal wood, ce-dar wood, and sweet white wine.
23
f
State-ly Span-ish gal-leon com-ing from the Isth-mus, Dip-
State-ly Span-ish gal-leon com-ing from the Isth-mus, Dip-
State-ly Span-ish gal-leon, Dip-
div. unis.
State-ly Span-ish gal-leon com-ing from the Isth-mus,

27
- - ping through the tro - pics by the palm - green shores, With a
- ping through the tro - pics by the palm - green shores, With a
- - ping through the tro - pics by the palm - green shores, With a
dip - ping through the tro - pics by the palm - green shores, With a
27
31
car - go of di - a - monds, em - - er - alds, am - e - thysts,
car - go of di - a - monds, em - er - alds, am - e - thysts,
car - go of di - a - monds, em - er - alds, am - e - thysts,
car - go of di - a - monds, em - - er - alds, am - - - e - thysts,
31
35
To - paz - es, and cin - na - mon, and gold moi - - dores.
To - paz - es, and cin - na - mon, and gold moi - dores.
To - paz - es, and cin - na - mon, and gold moi - dores.
To - paz - es, and cin - na - mon, and gold moi - - - dores.
(sost.)
div.
35

40
Più allegro (♩=152)
p
Dir - ty Brit - ish coast - er with a salt - caked smoke stack, But - ting through the
45
cresc.
ff
chan - nel in the mad March days, With a car - - - - - - go of
50
Tyne coal, road - rails, pig - lead, Fire - wood, i - ron ware, and
mf

55
Tempo primo
State - ly Span - ish
Quin - que - reme of Nin - e - veh from dis - tant
(Hum)
trays. (Hum)
div.
cheap tin trays. (Hum)
55
Tempo primo
60
Molto allegro
dim. e rit.
gal - leon. (Hum.)
Dir - ty Brit - ish coast - er with a salt - caked smoke stack.
O - phir. (Hum.)
Dir - ty Brit - ish coast - er with a salt - caked smoke stack.
Dir - ty Brit - ish coast - er with a salt - caked smoke stack.
Dir - ty Brit - ish coast - er with a salt - caked smoke stack.
60
Molto allegro

*In memory of my mother*

# 5. CELANDINE

(No.6 of *The Sun on the Celandines*)

Text
Edward Thomas

ROBERT WALKER
(b. 1946)

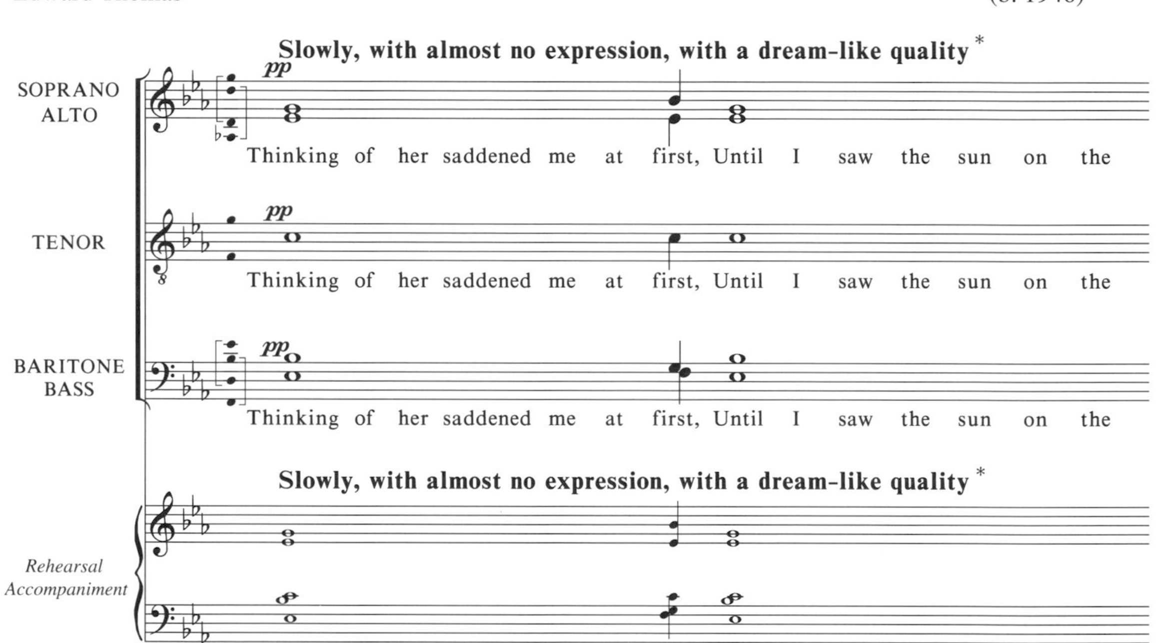

* Each quaver/syllable about mm112 but this should be infinitely variable depending upon the flow and sense of the words.

As before
p
liv-ing thing, not what be-fore I'd nursed, The shadow I was growing to love
As before
poco dim.
al-most The phantom, not the creature with bright eye That I had thought never to
As before
pp
see, once lost. She found the celandines of February Al-ways be-fore us all.

poco a poco cresc.
Her nature and name Were like those flowers, and now im-mediately, For a short swift
poco a poco cresc.
Her nature and name Were like those flowers, and now im-mediately, For a short swift
poco a poco cresc.
Her nature and name Were like those flowers, and now im-mediately, For a short swift
(f)
dim.
eternity back she came, Beau-ti-ful, hap-py, sim-ply as when
(f)
dim.
eternity back she came, Beau-ti-ful, hap-py, sim-ply as when
(f)
dim.
eternity back she came, Beau-ti-ful, hap-py, sim-ply as when
As before
pp
she wore Her brightest bloom among the winter hues Of all the world; and I was happy too,
pp
she wore Her brightest bloom among the winter hues Of all the world; and I was happy too,
pp
she wore Her brightest bloom among the winter hues Of all the world; and I was happy too,
As before

Seeing the blossoms and the maiden who Had seen them with me
Seeing the blossoms and the maiden who Had seen them with me
Seeing the blossoms and the maiden who Had seen them with me
Februarys before, Bend-ing to them as in and out she trod And laughed, with locks
Februarys before, Bend-ing to them as in and out she trod And laughed, with locks
Februarys before, Bend-ing to them as in and out she trod And laughed, with locks
As before, slightly slower
p' pp
sweep-ing the moss-y sod. But this was a dream: the flowers were not true,
p' pp
sweep-ing the moss-y sod. But this was a dream: the flowers were not true,
p' pp
sweep-ing the moss-y sod. But this was a dream: the flowers were not true,
As before, slightly slower

Until I stooped to pluck from the grass there One of five pe-tals
Until I stooped to pluck from the grass there One of five pe-tals
Until I stooped to pluck from the grass there One of five pe-tals
p
and I smelt the juice which made me sigh, remembering she was no more,
p
and I smelt the juice which made me sigh, remembering she was no more,
p
and I smelt the juice which made me sigh, remembering she was no more,
rit.
dim.
pp
Gone like a ne - ver per - fect - ly re - called dream.
pp
Gone like a ne - ver per - fect - ly re - called dream.
pp
Gone like a ne - ver per - fect - ly re - called dream.
rit.

# 6. COME AWAY, COME AWAY, DEATH

Text
William Shakespeare

GEORGE ALEXANDER MACFARREN
(1813 - 1887)

10

-way, fly a-way, *f* breathe; I am *pp* slain by a

-way, fly a-way, *f* breathe; I am *pp* slain by a

*cresc.* fly a-way, fly a-way, *f* breathe; I *unis. mf* am slain. I am slain by a

*cresc.* fly a-way, fly a-way, *f* breathe; I am *pp* slain. by a

10

15

fair cru-el maid. *pp dolce* My shroud of white stuck all with yew, my shroud, O pre-

fair cru-el maid. *pp dolce* My shroud of white stuck all with yew, my shroud, O pre-

fair cru-el maid. *div. pp dolce* My shroud of white stuck all with yew, my shroud, O pre-

fair cru-el maid. *pp dolce* My shroud of white stuck all with yew, O pre-

15

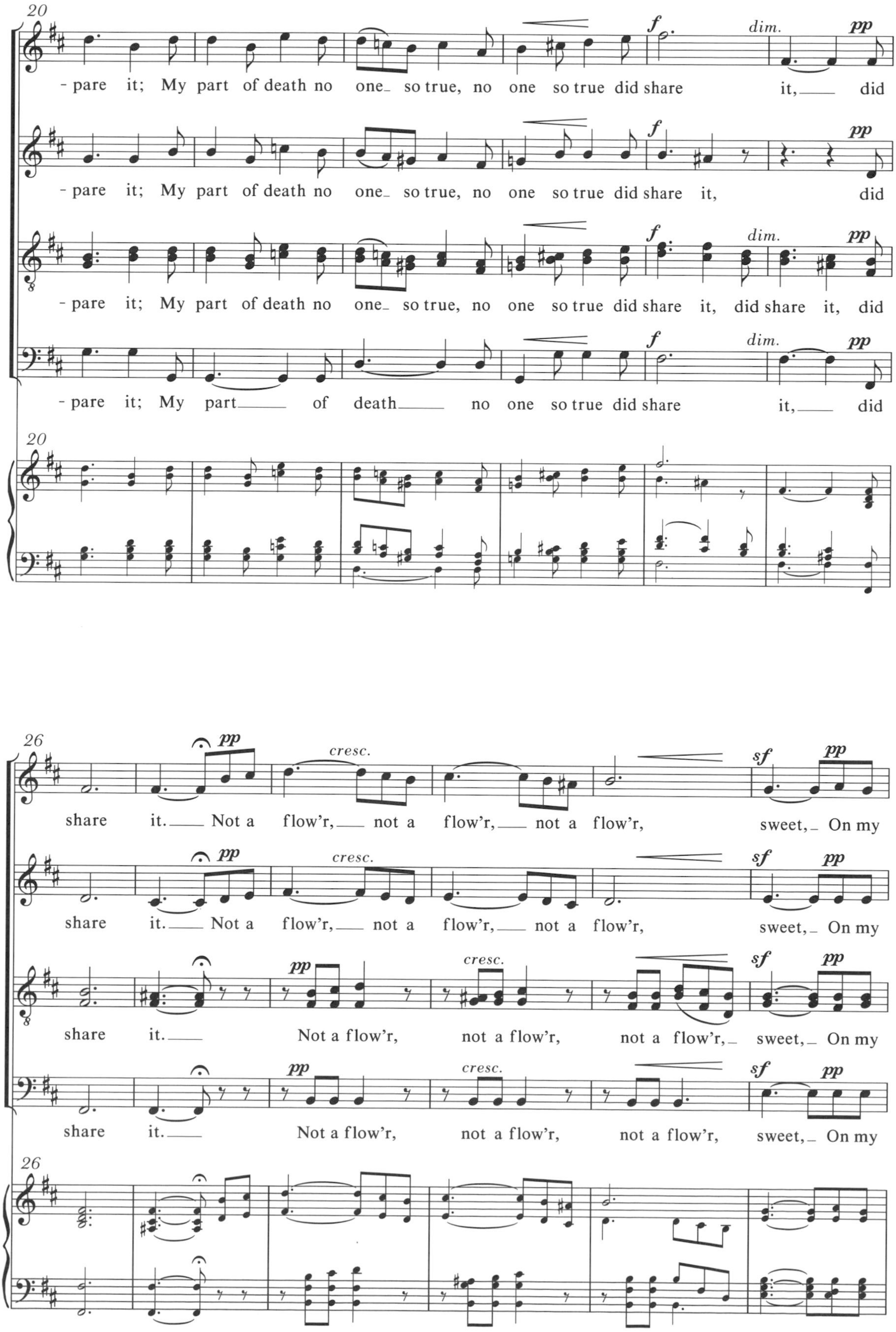
20
f
dim.
pp
-pare it; My part of death no one_ so true, no one so true did share it,___ did
f
pp
-pare it; My part of death no one_ so true, no one so true did share it, did
f
dim.
pp
-pare it; My part of death no one_ so true, no one so true did share it, did share it, did
f
dim.
pp
-pare it; My part___ of death___ no one so true did share it,___ did
20
26
pp
cresc.
sf
pp
share it.___ Not a flow'r,___ not a flow'r,___ not a flow'r, sweet,_ On my
pp
cresc.
sf
pp
share it.___ Not a flow'r,___ not a flow'r,___ not a flow'r, sweet,_ On my
pp
cresc.
sf
pp
share it.___ Not a flow'r, not a flow'r, not a flow'r,_ sweet,_ On my
pp
cresc.
sf
pp
share it.___ Not a flow'r, not a flow'r, not a flow'r, sweet,_ On my
26

32
pp
cresc.
black cof-fin let there be strown; Not a friend, not a friend, not a
black cof-fin let there be strown; Not a friend, not a friend, not a
black cof-fin let there be strown; Not a friend, not a friend,
black cof-fin let there be strown; Not a friend, not a friend,
38
f
pp
mf
sf
p
friend greet My poor corpse, where my bones shall be thrown: A
friend greet My poor corpse, where my bones shall be thrown: A
not a friend greet My poor corpse, where my bones shall be thrown: A
not a friend greet My poor corpse, where my bones shall be thrown:

44

*sf* *sf* *pp*

thou - sand thou - sand sighs to save, Lay me, lay me,

*sf* *sf*

thou - sand thou - sand sighs to save,

*sf* *sf* *pp*

thou - sand thou - sand sighs to save, Lay me, lay me,

*pp*

Lay me, lay me,

44

50

*pp*

lay me, O, where Sad true lov - er ne'er find my grave, To

*pp*

O where, To

where, where sad true lov - er ne'er find my grave

div. *f* *p*

lay me where Sad true lov - er ne'er find my grave, To

*pp*

lay me where, O where,

50

56

sf sf sf

weep there, — where sad true lov - er ne'er find my grave, — ne'er find — my

sf sf sf

weep there, — where sad true lov - er ne'er find my grave, — ne'er find — my

pp pp sf sf

weep there, — To weep there, — where sad true lov - er ne'er find my grave, — ne'er find — my

pp sf sf

To weep there, — where sad true lov - er ne'er find my grave, — ne'er find — my

56

65

sf pp pp

grave, — To weep there, — to weep — there, — to weep — there. —

sf pp pp

grave, — To weep — there, — to weep there, — to weep — there. —

weep — weep

sf pp pp

grave, — To weep — there, — to weep — there, — to weep — there. —

sf pp pp

grave, — To weep there, — to weep there, — to weep — there. —

65

# 7. COME LET US JOIN THE ROUNDELAY

Text
Anon.

WILLIAM BEALE
(1784 - 1854)
Edited by Robert Walker

Originally written for male voices.

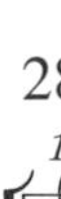

11

la la la la la la la la, Fa la la la la la la, [f] While the Fauns,

la la la la la la la la la, Fa la, la la la la, [f] While the Fauns, while the

la la la la Fa la la, Fa la la la la, [f] While the Fauns and Sa-tyrs

Fa la la la la, Fa la la la la la, [f] While the Fauns,

17

while the Fauns and Sa-tyrs round, [dim. poco a poco] Dance a-long on fai-

Fauns and Sa-tyrs round, while the Fauns and Sa-tyrs round, [dim. poco a poco] Dance a-long on

round, the Fauns and Sa-tyrs Dance a-long, [dim. poco a poco] dance a-long on fai - - - ry

while the Fauns and Sa-tyrs [dim. poco a poco] Dance a-long on fai-ry, fai-

23

-ry 1 [p] ground. 2 [p] ground, And the mer-ry nymphs and [< f] swains Gai-ly trip these ru-ral

fai-ry [p] ground. [p] ground, And the mer-ry nymphs and [< f] swains Gai-ly trip these ru-ral

fai-ry [p] ground. [p] ground, And the mer-ry nymphs and [< f] swains Gai-ly trip these ru-ral

-ry [p] ground. [p] ground, And the mer-ry nymphs and [< f] swains Gai-ly trip these ru-ral

29
[mp]
plains. Fa la la la la la la, Fa la la la
plains. Fa la la la la la la, Fa la la la la, Fa la
plains. Fa la la la la, Fa la la la la, Fa la la la la
plains. Fa la la la la la la, Fa la la la la la la
29
33
[cresc. poco a poco]
la la la, Fa la la la la la la, Fa la la la la, Fa la la la la, Fa la
la la la la la, Fa la la la la la la la, Fa la la la la la la la la la
la la la la, Fa la la la la la la la la la, Fa la la la la la
la la la la la, Fa la la la la, Fa la la la la, Fa la la la la
33
37
[f]
[p]
la, Fa la la la la la, And the mer - ry nymphs and swains Gai - ly
la, Fa la la la la la, And the mer - ry nymphs and swains Gai - ly
la, Fa la la la la la, And the mer - ry nymphs and swains Gai - ly
la, Fa la la la la la, And the mer - ry nymphs and swains Gai - ly
37

43
[pp]
trip these ru - ral plains. Fa la la la la la la,
[pp]
trip these ru - ral plains. Fa la la la, Fa la la la, Fa la
[pp]
trip these ru - ral plains. Fa la la la la, Fa la la la
[pp]
trip these ru - ral plains. Fa la la la la la la,
43
47
[cresc. poco a poco]
Fa la la la la la la, Fa la la la la la la, Fa la
[cresc. poco a poco]
la la la, Fa la la la la la la, Fa la la, Fa la la la
[cresc. poco a poco]
la, Fa la la la la la la la la, Fa la la la
[cresc. poco a poco]
Fa la la la la la la la la la la la, Fa la la la la,
47
50
[,] [ff]
la la la, Fa la la la la, Fa la la, Fa la la la la la.
[,] [ff]
la, Fa la la la la la la la la la la, Fa la la la la la.
[,] [ff]
la la la la la la, Fa la la la la la la, Fa la la la la la.
[,] [ff]
Fa la la la la, Fa la la la la la, Fa la la la la la.
50

# 8. COME LIVE WITH ME

Text
Christopher Marlowe

W. STERNDALE BENNETT
(1816 - 1875)

8
dim.
p
field, And all the crag - gy moun-tains yield. There will we sit up-on the
field, And all the crag - gy moun-tains yield. There will we sit up-on the
field, And all the crag - gy moun-tains yield. There will we sit up-on the
field, And all the crag - gy moun-tains yield. There will we
12
ca - lan - do sempre
rocks, And see the shep - herds feed their flocks, By shal-low ri - vers, to whose
rocks, And see the shep - herds feed their flocks, By shal-low ri - vers, to whose
rocks, And see the shep-herds feeds their flocks, By shal-low ri - vers, to whose
sit up - on the rocks, By shal - low ri-vers, to whose
16
pp
f
falls Me - lo-dious birds sing ma - dri-gals. And if these plea - sures may thee
falls Me - lo-dious birds sing ma - dri-gals. And if these plea - sures may thee
falls Me-lo-dious birds sing ma-dri-gals. And if these plea - sures may thee
falls Me - lo-dious birds sing ma - dri-gals. And if these plea - sures may thee

20
ff
move, Then live with me, and be my love, And if these plea - sures may thee
ff
move, Then live with me, and be my love, And if these plea - sures may thee
ff
move, Then live with me, and be my love, And if these plea - sures may thee
ff
move, Then live with me, and be my love, And if these plea - sures may thee
20
24
dim.
p
f
move, Then live with me, and be my love then live with me,
dim.
p
f
move, Then live with me, and be my love, then live with me,
dim.
p
move, Then live with me, and be my love,
dim.
p
f
move, Then live with me, and be my love, Then live, then
24
28
and be my love, then live with me,
and be my love, then live with me,
f
then live with me, and be my love,
f
live, then live with me, and be my love, then live with
28

32
and be my love. There will I make thee beds of
and be my love. There will I make the beds of
then live with me, and be my love. There will I make the beds of
me, then live with me, and be my love. There will I make the beds of
f
36
ros - es, With a thou - sand fra - grant po - sies, A cap of flow - ers and a
40
kir - tle, a cap of flow - ers, and a kir - tle Em - broi - der'd all with leaves of
kir - tle, cap of flow - ers, and a kir - tle Em - broi - der'd all with leaves of
dim.

44
p
myr-tle; The shep-herd swains shall dance and sing For thy de - light, each May morn-
p
myr-tle; The shep-herd swains shall dance and sing For thy de - light, each May morn-
p
myr-tle; The shep-herd swains shall dance and sing For thy de-light, each May morn-
p
myr-tle, The shep - - - herd swains shall dance and
44
48
ca - lan - do sempre pp
-ing, The shep-herd swains shall dance and sing For thy de-light, each
ca - lan - do sempre pp
-ing The shep-herd swains shall dance and sing For thy de-light, each
ca - lan - do sempre pp
-ing, The shep-herd swains shall dance and sing For thy de - light each May morn-
ca - lan - do sempre pp
sing, The shep - herd swains shall sing For thy de-light, each
48
52
f
May morn-ing; If these de - lights thy mind may move, Then live with me, and be my
f
May morn-ing; If these de - lights thy mind may move, Then live with me, and be my
f
-ing; If these de - lights thy mind may move, Then live with me, and be my
f
May morn-ing; If these de - lights thy mind may move, Then live with me, and be my
52

56
love, If these de - lights thy mind may move, Then live with me, and be my
love, If these de - lights thy mind may move, Then live with me, and
love, If these de - lights thy mind may move, Then live with me, and
love, If these de - lights thy mind may move, Then live with me, and
ff
dim.
p
56
60
love, then live with me, and be my
be my love, then live with me, and be my
be my love, then live with me, and be my
be my love, then live, then live, then live with me, and be my
f
60
64
love, then live with me, and be my love.
love, then live with me, and be my love.
love, then live with me, and be my love.
love, then live with me, then live with me, and be my love.
f
64

*To C.H. Lloyd*

# 9. CUPID AND ROSALIND

(No.4 from the second set of *Six Elizabethan Pastorals*)

Text
Thomas Lodge

C.V. STANFORD

20
mp
And if I sleep, then perch - eth he, With pret - ty slight, And makes a pil - low
mp

24
p
of my knee, The live-long night. Strike I my lute, he tunes the string;
p

29
He lends me ev-'ry love - - ly
p
He mu - sic plays if I but sing; He lends me ev-'ry love-ly
p
p

34
cresc.
f
p
thing, Yet cru - el he my heart doth sting. Whilst, wan - ton, still ye!
cresc.
f
p

39
f
Else I with ro - ses ev - 'ry day will whip ye hence, And bind ye,
f

44
ff
mf
cresc.
div.
when ye long to play, For your of - fence. I'll shut my eyes to keep ye in, I'll
ff
mf
div.
cresc.

49
f
make you fast it for your sin, I'll count your power not worth a pin.
f

53
poco rall.
a tempo
unis.
p
f
A - las! what here - by shall I win If he gain - say me? What if I beat the
unis.
p
f

58
wan - ton boy With ma-ny a rod? He will re-pay me with an - noy, Be-

62
p legato
- cause a god. Then sit thou safe - ly on my knee, And let thy
And let thy
div.
unis.
div.
unis.
p legato

67
Lurk in my eyes, I like of
bower my bo-som be; Lurk in my eyes, I like of
And let thy bower my bo-som be,

73
rall.
O Cu-pid! so thou
a tempo
mf
p
thee. O Cu-pid! so thou pi - ty me, Spare not, but play thee.
mf
mf
mf
p

# 10. ECHOES

Text
Thomas Moore

ARTHUR SULLIVAN
(1842 - 1900)

22
Goes an - sw'ring
far a-way o'er lawns and lakes, Goes an-sw'ring light, Goes an - sw'ring light!

p
28
Yet love hath e-choes tru - er far, And far more sweet Than
p

33
cresc.
The songs re -
f
e'er be-neath the moon-light's star, Of horn, or lute, or soft gui-tar, The songs re -
f
cresc.
f

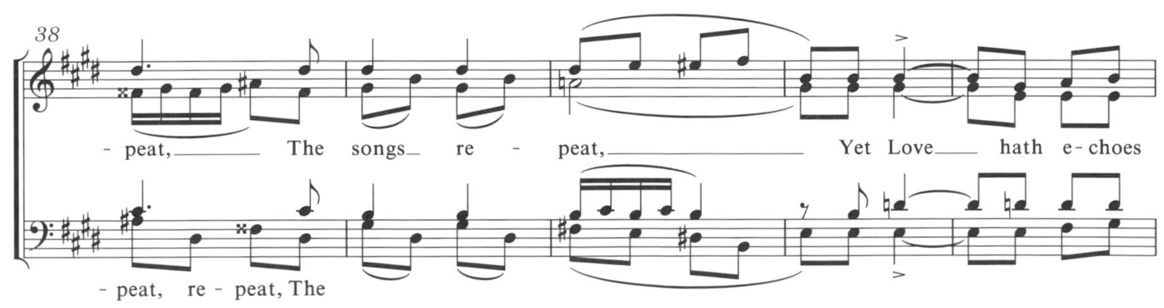
38
- peat, The songs re - peat, Yet Love hath e-choes
- peat, re - peat, The

43
dim.
p
staccato
tru - er far, And far more sweet, Than e'er be-neath the moon-light's_ star, Of
dim.
p
staccato

49
The_ songs___ re - peat.
horn, or lute, or soft_ gui - tar, The songs_ re - peat,_The songs re - peat.

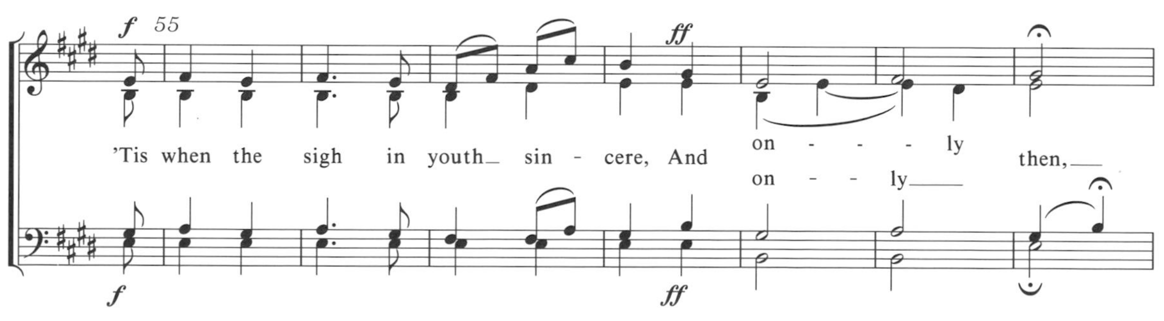
f 55
ff
'Tis when the sigh in youth_ sin - cere, And on - - - ly then,__
on - - ly___
f
ff

62
p
cresc.
f
The sigh that's breath'd for one_ to_ hear Is by that one, that on - ly_ Dear, Breath'd_
p
cresc.

67
back a - gain,
Breath'd back a - gain, Breath'd back a - gain, 'Tis when
a - gain,

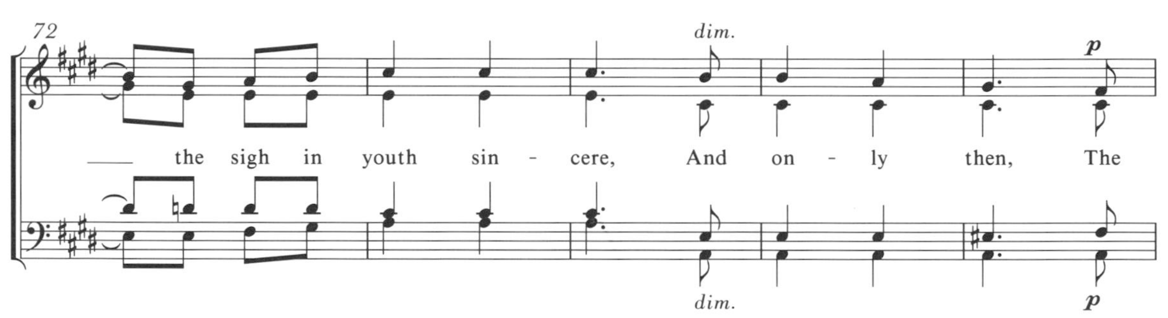
72
dim.
p
the sigh in youth sin - cere, And on - ly then, The
dim.
p

77
staccato
sigh that's breath'd for one to hear Is by that one, that on - ly Dear, Is
staccato

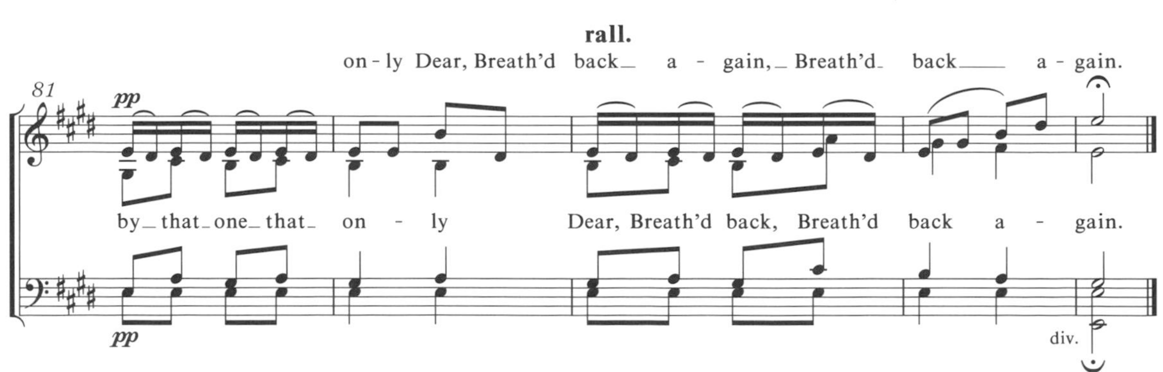
rall.
on - ly Dear, Breath'd back a - gain, Breath'd back a - gain.
81
pp
by that one that on - ly Dear, Breath'd back, Breath'd back a - gain.
pp
div.

# 11. EVENING HAS LOST HER THRONE

Text
Alfred Hayes

GRANVILLE BANTOCK
(1868 - 1946)

7

*cresc.* *dim.* *p*

ro-sy smile Fades from her dis-en-chant - - ed realms; Now dark - er sha - dows

*cresc.* *dim.* *p*

ro-sy smile Fades from her dis-en-chant - ed realms; Now dark-er sha-dows length-en from the

*cresc.* *dim.* *p*

Fades from her dis-en - chant - - ed realms; Now dark-er sha-dows

*dim.* *p*

realms; dis-en-chant-ed realms; Now dark-er sha - - dows

7

10

**rall.**

*dim.* *pp*

length-en from the file, length-en from the file Of loft-y dream - ing elms; The

*dim.* *pp*

file Of loft - y, loft - y dream - ing elms; The

*cresc.* *dim.* *pp*

length - en, length-en from the file, the file of loft-y dream-ing elms; The

*dim.* *pp*

length-en from the file Of loft - - - - y dream - ing elms; The

10

**rall.**

13 **Poco tranquillo**

*mp*

fields lie si-lent, wait-ing for the love Of yon-der moon, who lin-gers pale, Like a young

div. unis. *mp*

fields lie si-lent, wait-ing for the love Of yon - der moon, who

*mp*

fields lie si-lent, wait-ing for the love Of yon-der moon, who lin - gers

*mp*

fields lie si-lent, wait-ing for the love Of yon - der moon, who

13 **Poco tranquillo**

16
dim.
bride who lin - gers pale, like a young bride who lin - gers pale, Like a young bride be - hind her scarce - seen
dim.
lin - gers pale, Like a young bride be - hind her
dim.
pale, like a young bride who lin - gers pale, like a young bride who lin - gers pale be - hind her scarce - seen
dim.
lin - gers pale, Like a young bride be - hind her scarce - seen
19
pp
p
veil, Faint with sweet ea - ger - ness, yet shy To leave her mo - ther -
scarce - seen veil, Faint with ea - ger - ness, sweet ea - ger -
veil, Faint with ea - ger - ness, sweet ea - ger -
veil, be - hind her veil, Faint with sweet ea - ger - ness, yet shy To
22
p
- grove, to leave the bo - som of her mo - ther - grove, Faint with sweet ea - ger - ness, yet
- ness, yet shy To leave her mo - ther - grove, Faint with ea - ger -
- ness, yet shy To leave her mo - ther - grove, Faint with ea - ger -
leave the bo - som of her mo - ther - grove, Faint with sweet

25
poco rall.
dim.
shy To leave her mo-ther - grove, yet shy to leave the bo-som of her mo-ther-
- ness, sweet ea - - ger-ness, yet shy To leave the bo - som of her
dim.
- ness, sweet ea - - ger-ness, yet shy To leave the bo - som of her
dim.
ea - ger-ness, yet shy To leave the bo - som of her
dim.
25
poco rall.
28
p
- grove, to leave the bo-som of her mo-ther-grove And bare her bright-ness to the lone-ly
mo - ther - grove And
mo - ther - grove, her mo-ther-grove
mo - ther - grove
28
31
dim.
morendo
pp
sky.
p
bare her bright-ness to the lone-ly sky.
dim.
morendo
pp
p
And bare her bright-ness to the lone-ly sky.
morendo
pp
p
morendo
pp
And bare her bright-ness to the lone-ly sky.
31

*For David James and the New London Singers*

# 12. FRUIT MACHINE

(from *Three London Songs*)

Text
John Fuller

BRYAN KELLY
(b. 1934)

8

*pp* *f*

means, — my means: I've tried the dogs and dan - ces, And now it's the fruit ma -

*pp* *f*

means, — my means: I've tried the dogs and dan - ces, And now it's the fruit ma -

*pp* *f*

means, — my means: I've tried the dogs and dan - ces, And now it's the fruit ma -

*pp* *f*

means, — my means: I've tried the dogs and dan - ces, And now it's the fruit ma -

8

12

*mf legato*

- chines. From New Cross Gate to Dept - ford — The fruit is

*mf legato*

- chines. From New Cross Gate to Dept - ford — The fruit is

div. *mf legato* *simile*

- chines. New Cross Gate to Dept - ford, Dept - ford, New Cross

*mf legato* *simile*

- chines. New Cross Gate to Dept - -

12

18

**accel. poco a poco**

*staccato*

spin - ning fast, And as I range I save my change And

*staccato*

spin - ning fast, And as I range I save my change And

Gate to Dept-ford, Dept-ford, New Cross Gate to

-ford, Dept - - ford, New Cross Gate to

18

**accel. poco a poco**

23

**allegro molto**

*ff*

make the bit - ter last. O it's cher - ries and bells on Fri - day, On

*ff*

make the bit - ter last. cher - ries and bells on Fri - day, On

*ff staccato*

unis.

Dept - ford, Dept-ford, cher - ries and bells on Fri - day, on Fri - day,

*ff staccato*

Dept - ford, Dept - ford, cher - ries and bells on Fri - day, on Fri - day,

23

**allegro molto**

27

Sun - day it's plums and pears, pears, But pounds and jars and sev'ns and bars Means

Sun - day it's plums and pears, pears, But pounds and jars and sev'ns and bars Means

Sun - day it's plums and pears, pears, But pounds and jars and sev'ns and bars Means

Sun - day it's plums and pears, pears, But pounds and jars and sev'ns and bars Means

27

31

whoops up the Sat - ur - day, whoops up the Sat - ur - day, whoops up the Sat - ur - day stairs.

whoops up the Sat - ur - day, whoops up the Sat - ur - day, whoops up the Sat - ur - day stairs.

whoops up the Sat - ur - day, whoops up the Sat - ur - day, whoops up the Sat - ur - day stairs.

whoops up the Sat - ur - day, whoops up the Sat - ur - day, whoops up the Sat - ur - day stairs.

31

35
Tempo I
shoul- der
go round,
shoul- der
go round,
The girls hang on my shoulder To watch the fruit go round, I
The girls hang on my shoulder To watch the fruit go round, I
35
Tempo I
39
old - er
cer-tain-ly hold my
old - er
cer-tain-ly hold my
may be get-ting old - er But I cer-tain-ly hold my ground, And
may be get-ting old - er But I cer-tain-ly hold my ground, And
cresc.
39

43

ground, bold - er I stand an - o - ther

dim.

ground, bold - er I stand an - o - ther

dim.

if it makes them bold - er I stand an - o - ther round.

dim.

if it makes them bold - er I stand an - o - ther round.

dim.

43

3

3

47

mf legato

round. From New Cross Gate to Dept - ford The

mf legato

round. From New Cross Gate to Dept - ford The

div. mf simile

New Cross Gate to Dept - ford, Dept - ford

mf simile

New Cross Gate to

47

2

52
accel. poco a poco
staccato
beer is brown and deep, Just a veal-and-ham and a
beer is brown and deep, Just a veal-and-ham and a
New Cross Gate to Dept-ford, Dept-ford, New Cross
Dept - - ford, Dept - - ford, New Cross
57
allegro molto
ff staccato
unis.
Ba - by-cham Will make the dol - lies leap. Oh it's cher - ries and bells on
Ba - by-cham Will make the dol - lies leap. cher - ries and bells on
Gate to Dept - ford, Dept-ford, cher - ries and bells on
Gate to Dept - ford, Dept - ford, cher - ries and bells on

61
Fri-day, On Sun-day it's plums and pears, pears, But pounds and jars and sev'ns and bars Means
Fri-day, On Sun-day it's plums and pears, pears, But pounds and jars and sev'ns and bars Means
Fri-day, on Fri-day, Sun-day it's plums and pears, pears, But pounds and jars and sev'ns and bars Means
Fri-day, on Fri-day, Sun-day it's plums and pears, pears, But pounds and jars and sev'ns and bars Means
61
66
whoops up the Sat-ur-day, whoops up the Sat-ur-day, whoops up the Sat-ur-day stairs.
whoops up the Sat-ur-day, whoops up the Sat-ur-day, whoops up the Sat-ur-day stairs.
whoops up the Sat-ur-day, whoops up the Sat-ur-day, whoops up the Sat-ur-day stairs.
whoops up the Sat-ur-day, whoops up the Sat-ur-day, whoops up the Sat-ur-day stairs.
66

70
Tempo I
mf pp mf pp
The spin - ning fruit has wo - ken, wo - ken That child of dan - g'rous charm, charm
The spin - ning fruit has wo - ken, wo - ken That child of dan - g'rous charm, charm
The spin - ning fruit has wo - ken, wo - ken That child of dan - g'rous charm, charm
The spin - ning fruit has wo - ken, wo - ken That child of dan - g'rous charm, charm
70
Tempo I
74
mf pp mf pp f
Who lures me with a to - ken, to - ken And keeps me in a - larm, a - larm: My
Who lures me with a to - ken, to - ken And keeps me in a - larm, a - larm: My
Who lures me with a to - ken, to - ken And keeps me in a - larm, a - larm: My
Who lures me with a to - ken, to - ken And keeps me in a - larm, a - larm: My
74

78
en - ve - lope is bro - - ken To pull his ma - gic arm. From
en - ve - lope is bro - - ken To pull his ma - gic arm. From
en - ve - lope is bro - - ken To pull his ma - gic arm.
en - ve - lope is bro - - ken To pull his ma - gic arm.
78
82
mf legato
New Cross Gate to Dept - ford, Hap - p'ly
mf legato
New Cross Gate to Dept - ford, Hap - p'ly
div. mf
simile
New Cross Gate to Dept - ford, Dept - ford, New Cross
mf
simile
New Cross Gate to Dept - - -
82
87
accel. poco a poco
staccato
af - ter dark, When fruit falls thick I dance out quick With a
staccato
af - ter dark, When fruit falls thick I dance out quick With a
Gate to Dept - ford, Dept - ford, New Cross Gate to
- ford, Dept - - ford New Cross Gate to
87
accel. poco a poco

92
allegro molto
ff
girl in Green-wich Park. Oh it's cher - ries and bells on Fri - day, On
girl in Green-wich Park. cher - ries and bells on Fri - day, On
Dept - ford, Dept-ford, cher - ries and bells on Fri - day, on Fri - day,
unis.
Dept - ford, Dept - ford, cher - ries and bells on Fri - day, on Fri - day,
92
allegro molto
96
Sun - day it's plums and pears, pears, But pounds and jars and sev'ns and bars Means
Sun - day it's plums and pears, pears, But pounds and jars and sev'ns and bars Means
Sun - day it's plums and pears, pears, But pounds and jars and sev'ns and bars Means
Sun - day it's plums and pears, pears, But pounds and jars and sev'ns and bars Means
96
100
whoops up the Sat-ur-day, whoops up the Sat-ur-day, whoops, whoops,
whoops up the Sat-ur-day, whoops up the Sat-ur-day, whoops, whoops,
whoops up the Sat-ur-day, whoops up the Sat-ur-day, whoops, whoops,
whoops up the Sat-ur-day, whoops up the Sat-ur-day, whoops, whoops,
100

103
whoops up the Sat - ur - day, whoops, whoops, whoops, whoops up the Sat - ur - day,
whoops up the Sat - ur - day, whoops, whoops, whoops, whoops up the Sat - ur - day,
whoops up the Sat - ur - day, whoops, whoops, whoops, whoops up the Sat - ur - day,
whoops up the Sat - ur - day, whoops, whoops, whoops, whoops up the Sat - ur - day,
103
107
whoops up the Sat - ur - day, whoops up the Sat - ur - day stairs.
whoops up the Sat - ur - day, whoops up the Sat - ur - day stairs.
whoops up the Sat - ur - day, whoops up the Sat - ur - day stairs.
whoops up the Sat - ur - day, whoops up the Sat - ur - day stairs.
107

# 13. GO, LOVELY ROSE

9

**a tempo** *p* div. unis. **poco più mosso** *mp*

How sweet and fair she seems to be. Tell her that's young and

*p* *poco più mosso* *mp*

How sweet and fair she seems to be. Tell her that's young___ and

*p* div. unis. *poco più mosso* *mp*

How sweet and fair she seems to be. Tell her that's young___ and

*p* *poco più mosso* *mp*

How sweet and fair she seems to be. Tell her that's young and

9

**a tempo** **poco più mosso**

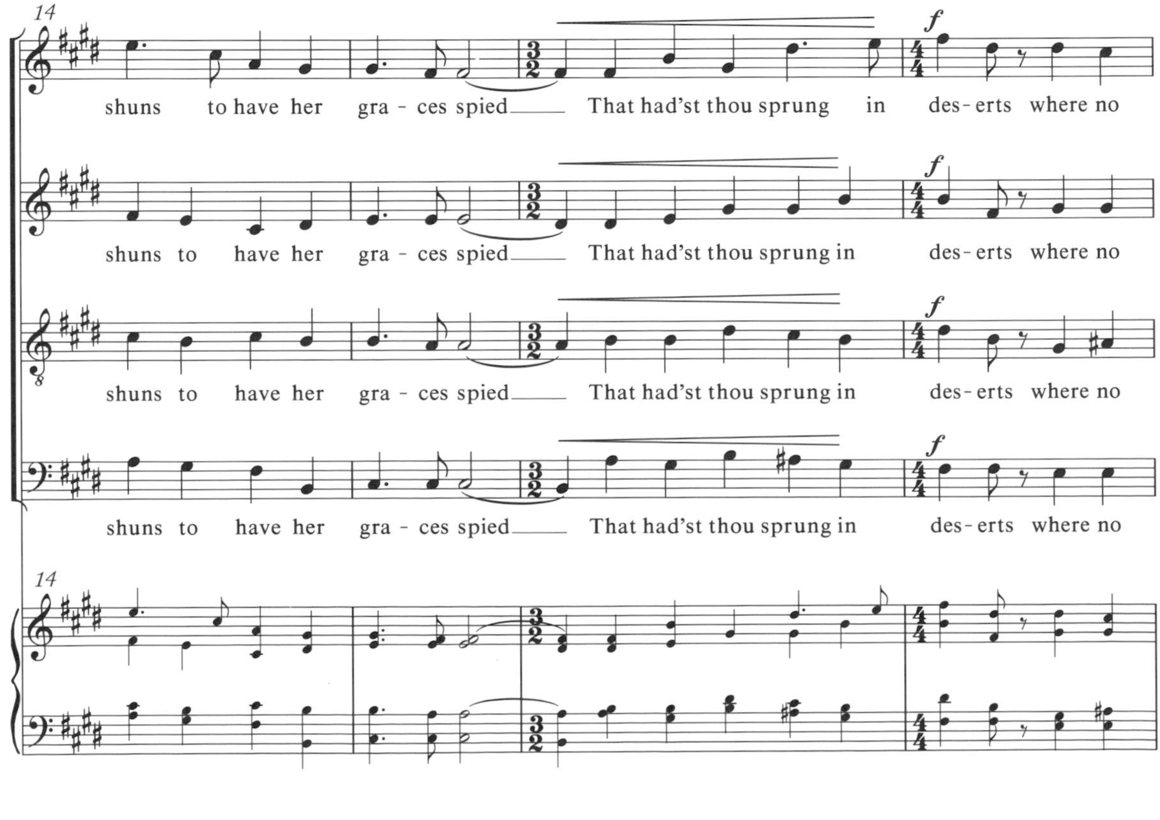

14

*f*

shuns to have her gra - ces spied___ That had'st thou sprung in des- erts where no

*f*

shuns to have her gra - ces spied___ That had'st thou sprung in des- erts where no

*f*

shuns to have her gra - ces spied___ That had'st thou sprung in des- erts where no

*f*

shuns to have her gra - ces spied___ That had'st thou sprung in des- erts where no

14

18
meno mosso
a tempo
pp
men a - bide Thou must have un - com - mend - - ed died.
men a - bide Thou must have un - com - mend - ed died.
men a - bide Thou must have un - com - mend - ed died.
men a - bide Thou must have un - com - mend - ed died.
22
mp dolce
Small is the worth Of beau - ty from the light re - tired:
div.
unis.
Small is the worth Of beau - ty from the light re - tired:
Small is the worth Of beau - ty from the light re - tired:
Small is the worth Of beau - ty from the light re - tired:

26

**rall.** *molto*

Bid her come forth, suf-fer her-self to be de - sired, Then die! that

Bid her come forth, suf-fer her-self to be de - sired, Then die! that

Bid her come forth, suf-fer her-self to be de - sired, Then die! that

Bid her come forth, suf-fer her-self to be de - sired, Then die! that

30

**rall.**

she the com-mon fate of all things rare May read in thee

she the com-mon fate of all things rare May read in thee

she the com-mon fate of all things rare May read in thee

she the com-mon fate of all things rare May read in thee

34

a tempo

*p*

How small a part of time they share That are so

*p*

How small a part of time they share That are so

*p*

How small a part of time they share That are so

*p*

How small a part of time they share That are so

34

a tempo

37

rall.

won-drous sweet and fair.

div. unis. *smorz.*

won-drous sweet and fair. That are so won-drous sweet and fair.

*smorz.*

won-drous sweet and fair. That are so won-drous sweet and fair.

*smorz.* div.

won-drous sweet and fair. That are so won-drous sweet and fair.

37

rall.

# 14. INHERITANCE

Text
Walter de la Mare

HERBERT HOWELLS
(1892 - 1983)

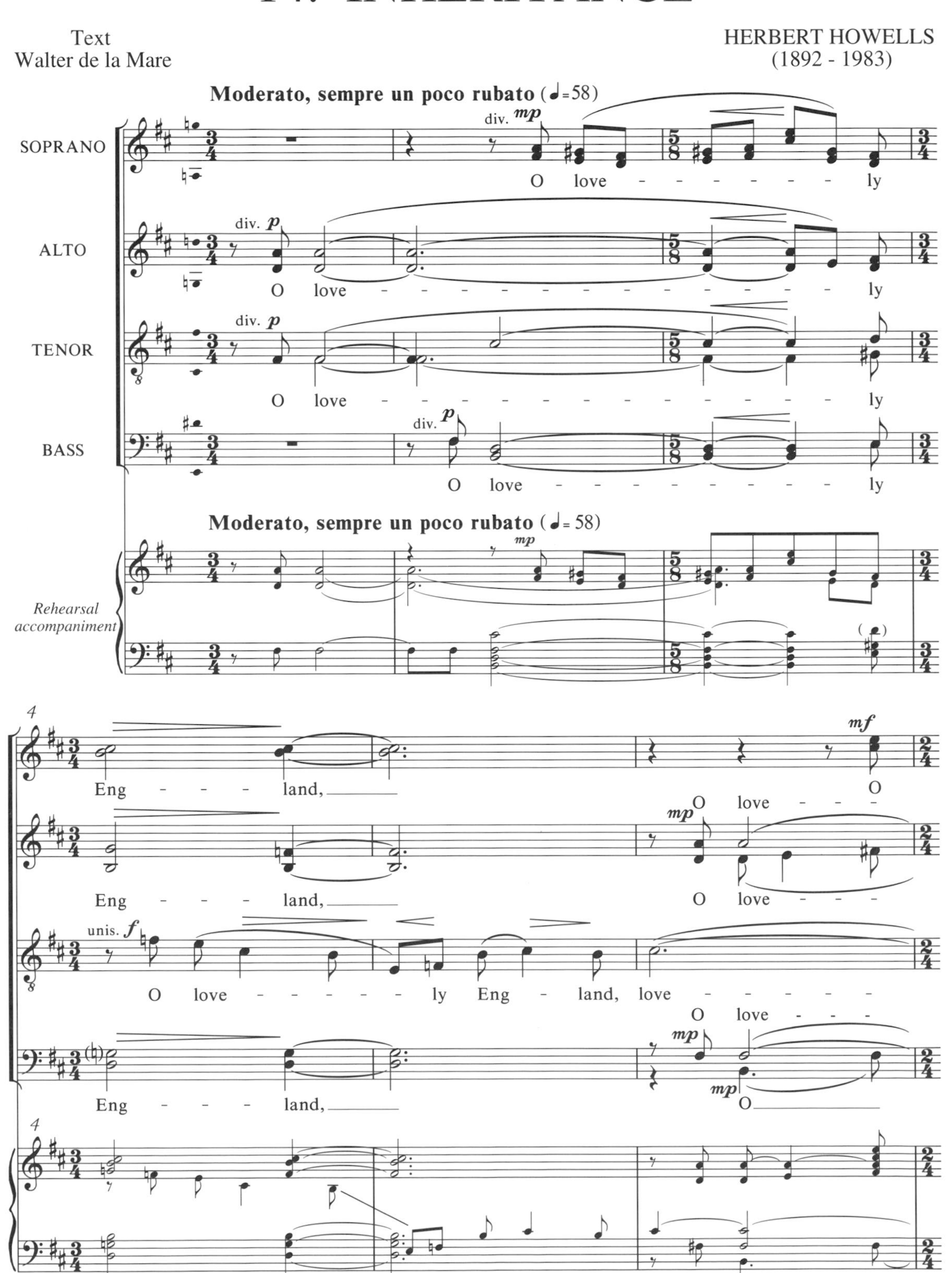

7
love - - - - - - - - - - - ly Eng - - land,
- - - - - - - - - - - - - ly,
poco
mf
- - - - - - - - - - - - - ly, O love - - - - - - ly
poco
- - - - - - - - - - - - - ly, love - - - - - - - - - - ly
- - - - - - - - - - - - - ly,
poco
unis.
love - - - - - - - - - - ly, love - - - - - - - - - - ly
7
11
unis.
cresc.
whose an - - - - - - - cient peace The di - - - rest dan -
cresc.
unis.
3
Eng - land, whose an - cient peace The di - - - - rest
cresc.
Eng - land, whose an - - cient peace The di - - - - - rest
cresc.
div.
unis.
Eng - - land, whose an - cient peace The di - - - - rest
11
3

14

*f* *più f*

- - - - - - gers fret, Be

div. unis. *f* *più f*

dan - - - gers fret, Be on the

*f*

dan - - - - gers fret,

*f* *più f*

dan - - - gers fret, Be on the

14

17

*dim.*

on the me - - mory of your past your sure de -

div. unis. *dim.*

me - - - - - - - - - mory of your past your de -

*più f* *dim.*

Be on the me- mory of your past your de -

*dim.*

me - - - - - - - - - mory of your past your sure de -

17

20
con anima
-vo - tion set;
Give
-vo - tion set;
Give still,
give
-vo - tion set;
Give still,
give still
div.
-vo - tion set;
Give still,
give still
div.
20
con anima
24
cresc. subito
still,
true free-dom to ful - fil,
Give
still
still,
true free-dom to ful - fil,
Give
still
div.
unis.
unis.
Give, still,
Give,
give
Give,
Give still,
true free-dom to ful - fil,
give
still
24

28

ff div. mp

your all, give still, give still your all with-

ff div. unis. mf espress.

your all, give still, give still your all with-

ff mp

your all, give still your all,

ff unis. mp

your all, give still your all

28

32

p

-out re - gret!

p unis.

-out re - gret! with-out re -

mf

give still your all with-out

div. p

with - out re -

32

35

**affrettando** (♩= 72)

unis.

Heed, through the trou - bles that be-

- gret! Heed, through the trou - bles that be-

re - gret! Heed, through the trou - bles that be-

unis.

- gret! Heed, through the trou - bles that be-

35

**affrettando** (♩= 72)

39

**più e più incalzando ed accel.**

numb Voi-ces now stilled, yet clear,

div.

numb Voi - - - ces now stilled, yet clear,

numb Voi - - - ces now stilled, yet clear,

numb Voi - - - ces now stilled, yet clear,

39

**più e più incalzando ed accel.**

42
div.
unis.
Chaunt - - - - - - - - - - ing their death - less songs– too oft To
unis.
Chaunt - - - - - - - - - - ing their death - - less songs– To
Chaunt - - - - - - - - - ing their songs– too oft To
Chaunt - - - - - - - - - ing their death - less songs– To
42
45 
(♩= 84)
ff elato
div.
ears that would not hear, Chaunt - ing,
ff elato
ears that would not hear, Chaunt - ing,
ff elato
ears that would not hear, Chaunt-ing,
ff elato
div.
ears that would not hear, Chaunt-ing,
45
(♩= 84)

48
unis.
div.
unis.
chaunt - - - - ing their death - less songs,-
chaunt - - - - ing their death - less songs,-
div.
unis.
chaunt - ing their
chaunt - - - - ing their death - less songs,-
chaunt - - -
unis.
div.
unis.
chaunt - - - - ing their death - less songs,-
chaunt - - - - - -
48
stringendo
51
div.
chaunt - - - - - - - - - - ing their
death - - - - - -
death - - - - - less
songs,
their
death - - - - - -
- - - - - - - ing, chaunt - - - ing their
death - - - - - - -
- - - - - - ing, chaunt - - ing their
death - - - - - -
stringendo
51

54

unis. *f* allarg. *ff*

- - - less songs Urg - ing you, so - -

*f* *ff*

- - - less songs Urg - ing you, urg - -

*f* div. *ff*

- - - less songs Urg - ing you, so - -

*ff*

- - - - - - less songs Urg - ing, urg - -

54

allarg.

58

ritardando

dim. *f espress.*

- - - - - lemn, sweet, To meet your fate

dim. *f espress.*

- - - ing so - lemn, sweet, To meet your

unis. dim. *f espress.*

- - - - - - - lemn, so - - - lemn, sweet, To meet your

dim.

- ing you, so - - lemn, sweet,

58

ritardando

63
dim.
div.
unis.
p
lunga
pp
un - moved by fear.
fate un - moved by fear.
fate un - moved by fear.
mf espress.
To meet your fate un - moved by fear.
67
risvegliato
f
molto
ff
unis.
Earth's ar - dent life in - cites you

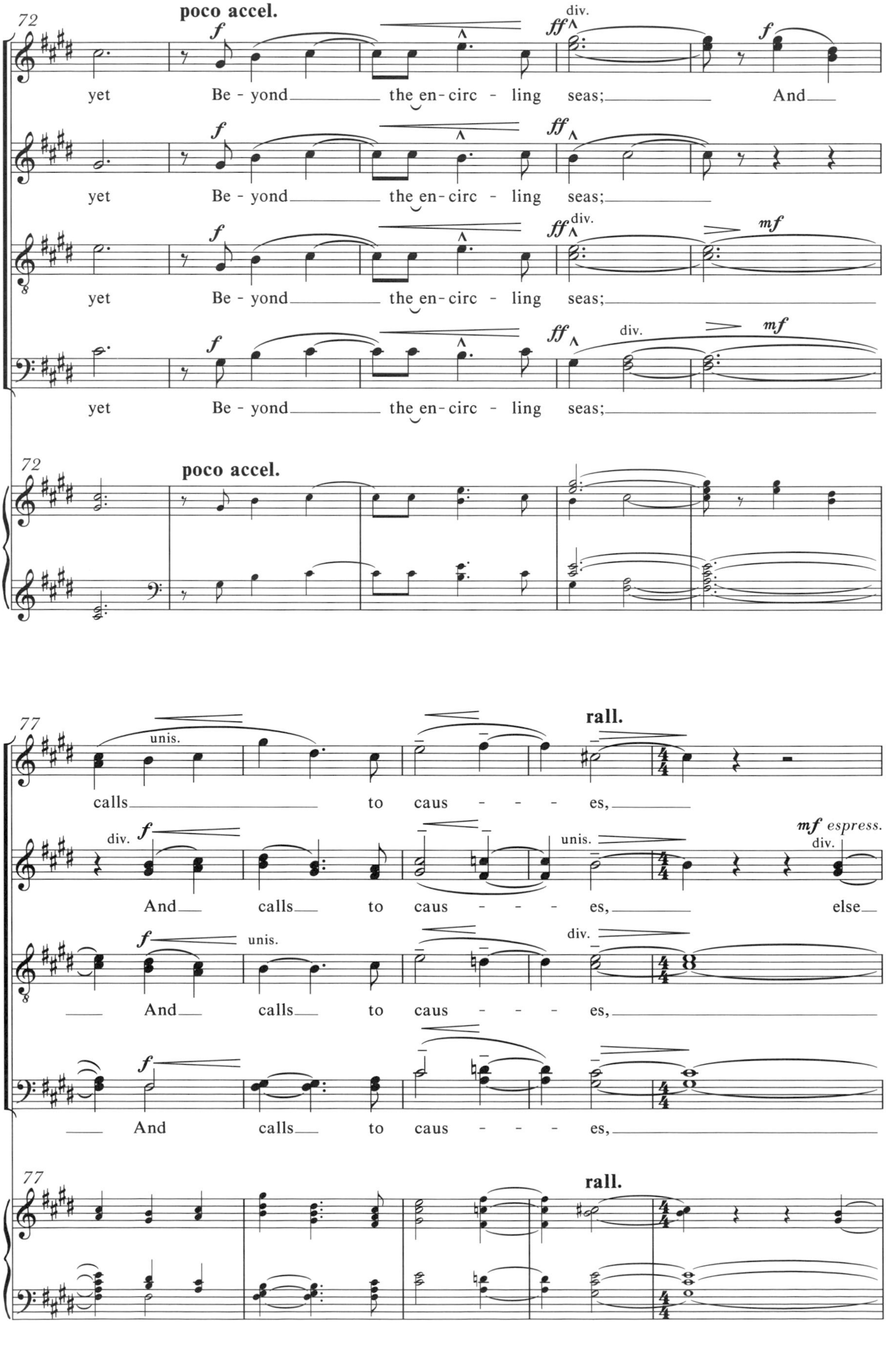

72
poco accel.
div.
yet Be - yond the en - circ - ling seas; And
yet Be - yond the en - circ - ling seas;
yet Be - yond the en - circ - ling seas;
yet Be - yond the en - circ - ling seas;
72
poco accel.
77
rall.
unis.
calls to caus - - - es,
mf espress.
div.
And calls to caus - - - es, else
unis.
And calls to caus - - - es,
And calls to caus - - - es,
77
rall.

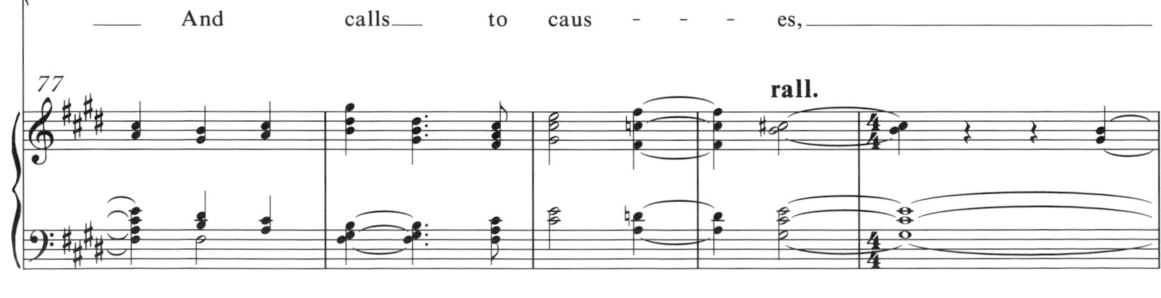

82
più rall. e perdendosi
p
else for - lorn,
3
for - lorn The chil - - - dren,
unis.
mf
else for - lorn The
mf
mp
else for - lorn, else
82
3
più rall. e perdendosi
86
p
estinto
div.
pp
else for - lorn The chil - dren at your knees.
unis.
p
div.
pp
else for - lorn The chil - dren at your knees.
ppp
chil - - - - - - - - - - - - - dren.
unis.
pp
for - lorn The chil - dren.
86
estinto

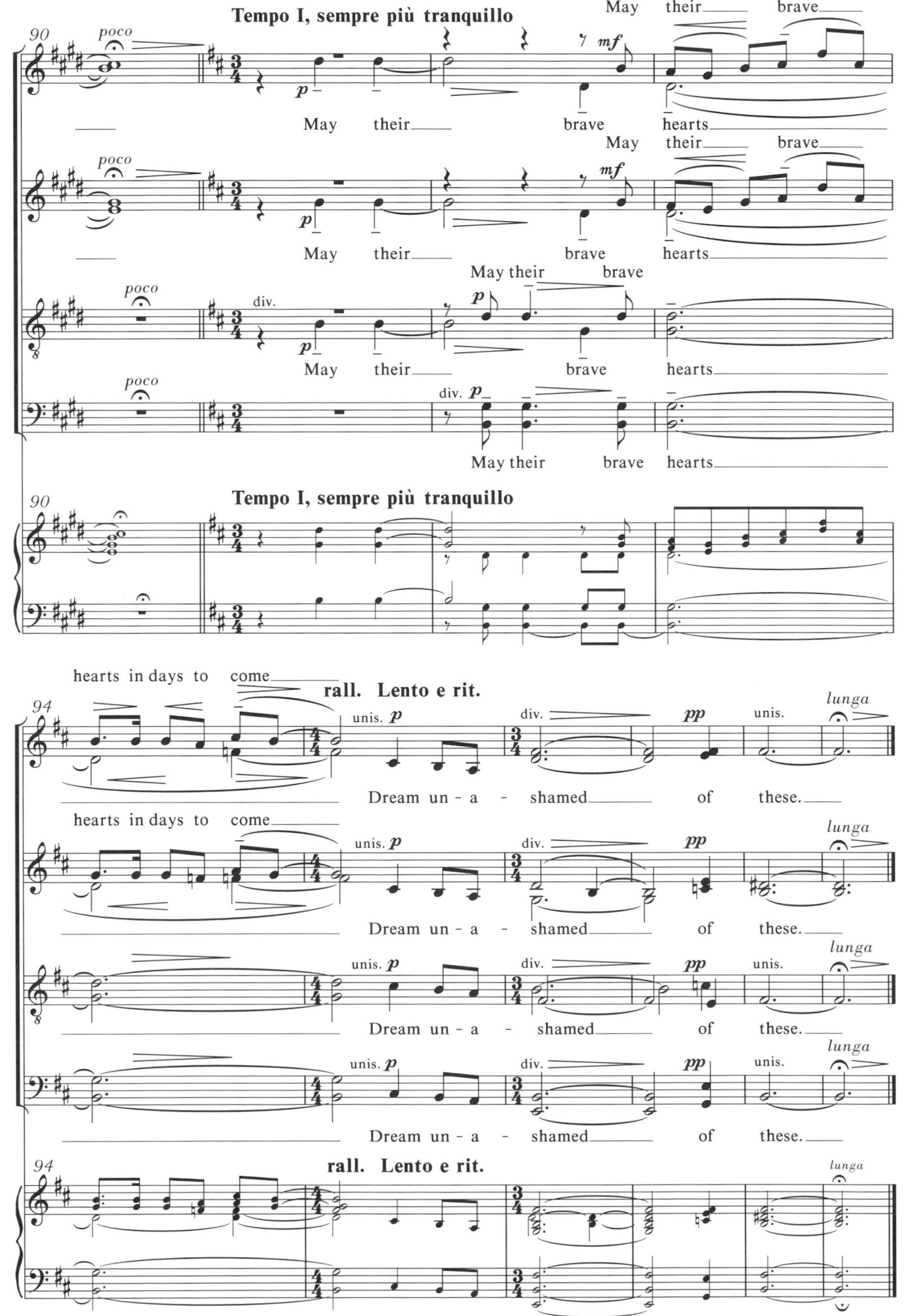
Tempo I, sempre più tranquillo
poco
May their brave hearts in days to come
div.
unis.
rall. Lento e rit.
Dream un - a - shamed of these.
lunga

# 15. IN THESE DELIGHTFUL, PLEASANT GROVES

From *The Libertine*

10
let us, let us sing, now let us, let us sing, re- joice, re- joice, re- joice and
let us, let us sing, now let us, let us sing, re- joice, re- joice, re- joice and
let us, let us sing, now let us, let us sing, re- joice, re- joice, re- joice and
let us, let us sing, now let us, let us sing, re- joice, re- joice, re- joice and
10
15
kiss, The great, the great can ne- ver, ne- ver, ne- ver know such
kiss, The great, the great can ne- ver, ne- ver, ne- ver know such
kiss, The great, the great can ne- ver, ne- ver, ne- ver know such
kiss, The great, the great can ne- ver, ne- ver, ne- ver know such
15
22
bliss as this, The great can ne- ver, ne- ver,
bliss as this, The great can ne- ver, ne- ver,
bliss as this, The great can ne- ver, ne- ver,
bliss as this, The great can ne- ver, ne- ver,
22

28
[♩. = 𝅗𝅥]
ne-ver know such bliss, can ne-ver, ne-ver, ne-ver know such bliss. In
ne-ver know such bliss, can ne-ver, ne-ver, ne-ver know such bliss. In
ne-ver know such bliss, can ne-ver, ne-ver, ne-ver know such bliss. In
ne-ver know such bliss, can ne-ver, ne-ver, ne-ver know such bliss. In
28
33
these de - light - ful, plea - sant groves, in these de - light - ful,
these de - light - ful, plea - sant groves, in these de - light - ful,
these de - light - ful, plea - sant groves, in these de - light - ful,
these de - light - ful, plea - sant groves, in these de - light - ful,
33
37
plea - - sant groves, Let us ce - le - brate, let us ce - le - brate, let us
plea - - sant groves, Let us ce - le - brate, let us ce - le - brate, let us
plea - sant groves, Let us ce - le - brate, let us ce - le - brate, let us
plea - - sant groves, Let us ce - le - brate, let us ce - le - brate, let us
37

41
ce - le - brate our hap - py, hap - py loves, In these de - light - ful,
ce - le - brate our hap - py, hap - py loves, In these de - light - ful,
ce - le - brate our hap - py, hap - py loves, In these de - light - ful,
ce - le - brate our hap - py, hap - py loves, In these de - light - ful,
41
45
plea - sant groves, in these de - light - ful, plea - sant groves, Let us
plea - sant groves, in these de - light - ful, plea - sant groves, Let us
plea - sant groves, in these de - light - ful, plea - sant groves, Let us
plea - sant groves, in these de - light - ful, plea - sant groves, Let us
45
50
ce - le - brate, let us ce - le - brate, let us ce - le - brate our
ce - le - brate, let us ce - le - brate, let us ce - le - brate our
ce - le - brate, let us ce - le - brate, let us ce - le - brate our
ce - le - brate, let us ce - le - brate, let us ce - le - brate our
50

53
hap - py, hap - py loves, Let's pipe, pipe and dance, let's
pipe, pipe and dance, dance and laugh, laugh,
pipe, pipe and dance, laugh, laugh, laugh,
57
61
laugh, laugh and sing; Thus,
laugh and sing, laugh and sing; Thus,

66
thus, thus ev - 'ry hap - py, hap - py liv - ing thing
thus, thus ev - 'ry hap - py, hap - py liv - ing thing Re -
thus, thus ev - 'ry hap - py, hap - py liv - ing thing Re -
thus, thus ev - 'ry hap - py, hap - py liv - ing thing
70
f
Re - vels in the cheer - ful Spring,
- vels in the cheer - ful, cheer - ful Spring, re -
- vels in the cheer - ful Spring, re -
Re - vels in the cheer - ful Spring,
75
re - vels in the cheer - ful Spring.
- vels in the cheer - ful, cheer - ful Spring.
- vels in the cheer - ful Spring.
re - vels in the cheer - ful Spring.

*Dedicated to Sir John and Lady Harington*

# 16. IN THIS HOUR OF SOFTENED SPLENDOUR

Text
Miss Horace Smith

CIRO PINSUTI
(1829 - 1888)

Con energia
In this hour, oh! La - dy, hear me, Bid me my pas - sion prove, With thy roy - al glance ah!
unis.
Con energia
cheer me, While I tell all my love, tell all my love,
con grazia
tell my love, tell my
cresc.
tell all my love, tell all my love, tell all my love, my
love, tell my love, tell all my love, my

24
p cresc. molto
rall.
dim.
a tempo
pp
love.
In this hour of soft - en'd splen - dour, When the
p div.
unis.
30
moon holds court on high,
f
Hear, Oh! hear me hom - age ren - der,
ff
And give me sigh for sigh,
for
div.
36
give sigh for sigh,
sigh,
for sigh.
for sigh,
for
sigh.
unis.

**Tempo primo**

43

See the gen - tle moon now pa - leth In the ra - diance of the dawn, And in

47

pure white robe she sail - eth, All her queen - ly glo - ries gone. In this hour, oh! La - dy,

**Con energia**

52

hear me, Bid me my pas - sion prove, With thy roy - al glance ah! cheer me,

57
p
While I tell all my love, tell all my love,
While I tell all my love, tell all my love,
con grazia
cresc.
While I tell all my love, tell my love, tell my
While I tell all my love, tell all my love,
57
61
cresc.
tell all my love,
f
tell all my love, tell all my
tell all my love, tell all my love, tell all my
love, tell my love, tell all my
tell all my love, tell all my love, tell all my
61
65
p
cresc. molto
rall.
dim.
a tempo
pp
love, my love. In this
love, my love. In this
love, my love. In this
love, my love. In this
65
rall.
a tempo

70
hour so soft and ten - der, When the moon for - gets to shine,
f
And the
unis.
70
74
cresc. molto
ff
dim.
p
day breaks forth in splen - dour, Say, say thou wilt be mine, thou wilt be
be mine, be mine,
div.
unis.
74
79
rall.
div.
pp
mine, be mine, be mine.
be mine.
79
rall.

# 17. INVOCATION TO SLEEP

Text
Beaumont and Fletcher

JULIUS BENEDICT
(1804 - 1885)

11
dim.
p
cresc.
sweet deceiving Lock me in de-
sweet de-ceiv-ing Lock me in de-
sweet de-ceiv-ing Lock me in de-light a-while, a-
sweet de-ceiv-ing Lock me in de-light a-
17
f
-light, in de-light, in de-light a-while;
-light, in de-light a-while; Let some
-while, in de-light a-while;
-while, in de-light a-while;
mf
23
cresc.
Let some pleas-ing dreams be-guile, let some
pleas-ing dreams be-guile, let some
Let some pleas-ing dreams, some
Let some

29
pleas - - - - - - ing dreams be - guile, some
pleas - ing dreams be - guile let some pleas - ing dreams,
pleas - - - - - - ing dreams, some dreams be -
cresc.
pleas - ing dreams, some dreams be - guile, let some
29
35
dreams, some pleas - ing dreams be - guile All my
let some pleas - ing dreams be - guile All my
- guile, let some dreams be - guile my
pleas - ing dreams, let some pleas - ing dreams be - guile my
35
41
fan - cies, be - guile all my fan - cies, that from thence,
fan - cies, be - guile, be - guile all fan - cies, that from
div.
unis.
fan - cies, be - guile all my fan - cies, that from
fan - cies, be - guile all my fan - cies,
41

48
cresc.
that from thence I may feel an influ -
cresc.
thence, from thence I may feel an in - flu -
cresc.
thence, from thence I may feel an in - flu -
pp
cresc.
that from thence I may feel an in - flu -
48
54
cresc.
- ence, All my pow - ers of care be - reav - - ing, all my pow - ers of
cresc.
- ence, All my pow'rs of care be - reav - - ing, all my pow - ers of
cresc.
- ence, All my pow - ers of care be - reav - - ing, all my pow - ers of
cresc.
- ence, All my pow'rs of care be - reav - - ing, all my pow - ers of
54
60
ff
f
care be - reav - ing, my pow'rs of care be -
ff
f
care be - reav - ing, my pow'rs of care be -
ff
f
care be - reav - ing, my pow'rs of care be -
ff
f
care be - reav - ing, my pow'rs of care be -
60

67
smorz.
-reav - - - - - ing.
smorz.
-reav - - - - - ing.
smorz.
-reav - - - - - ing. Though but a sha - dow,
smorz.
div.
unis.
-reav - - - - - ing. Though but a sha - dow,
67
74
Though but a sha - dow but a sli - ding,
Though but a sha - dow but a sli - ding,
but a sha - - - - - - dow, though but a sli - ding,
but a sha - - - - - - dow, though but a sli - ding,
74
81
Let me know some lit - - tle joy,
Let me know some lit - - tle joy,
Let me know some lit - - tle joy,
Let me know some lit - - tle joy,
81

89
ff
let me know some lit - - - - - tle joy,
let me know some lit - - tle joy,
let me know some lit - - - - - tle joy,
let me know some lit - - tle joy,
96
p
We that suf - - - - - - - fer long an - noy Are con -
We that suf - - fer long an - noy
We that suf - - fer long an - noy
We that suf - - - fer
cresc.
101
- tent - - - - - - ed with a thought, Through an i - - dle
Are con - tent - - ed with a thought, Through an i - - dle
Are con - tent - - ed with a thought, Through an i - - dle
Are con - tent - - ed with a thought, Through an i - - dle

106
fan - - cy wrought, Let my joys have some a -
fan - - cy wrought, Let my joys have some a -
fan - - cy wrought, Let my joys have some a -
fan - - cy wrought, Let my joys have some a -
106
111
ff f dim.
- bid - - ing, Oh, let my joys have some a -
- bid - - ing, Oh, let my joys have some a -
- bid - - ing, Oh, let my joys have some a -
- bid - - ing, Oh, let my joys have some a -
111
117
- bid - - - - - - - - - - - - - ing!
- bid - - - - - - - - - - - - - ing!
- bid - - - - - - - - - - - - - ing!
div.
- bid - - - - - - - - - - - - - ing!
117

# 18. JOHN COOK

Text
Anon.

THEA MUSGRAVE
(b. 1928)

Shu - ter's Bank, And there his nag
25
up Shu - ter's Bank, did
Shu - ter's Bank,
31
did kick and prank,
kick and prank, He, haw,
did kick and prank,
(nasal)
(nasal)
37
He, haw, hum!(m) He, haw, hum!(m) He, haw, hum!(m)
John Cook was ri - ding up
leggiero
43
up Shu - ter's Hill, His
Shu - ter's Hill, up Shu - ter's Hill,
49
mare fell down, down,
his mare fell down, down,
div.
(Bass) div.
And his

55
sfzp
down,
mare fell down
sfzp
f
and she made her will,
61
p legato
The bri - dle and sad -
68 - dle,
poco rall.
- dle were laid
were laid on the shelf,
p legato
75
a tempo
unis. p
If you want
He, haw, hum! (m) He, haw, hum! (m) He, haw,
pp
81
senza rall.
f
an - y more
you may make it your - self.
hum! (m) He, haw, hum! (m)
f

# 19. LAY A GARLAND

Text
Beaumont and Fletcher

ROBERT PEARSALL
(1795 - 1856)

6
cresc.
on her hearse Of dis - - - - - - - - - - mal yew;
p
hearse, Of dis - - - - mal yew;
cresc.
her hearse Of dis - mal yew;
cresc.
p
Of dis - - - - - - - - mal yew;
cresc.
p
p
Of dis - - - - - mal yew; Maid-
her hearse,
p
her hearse Of dis - - - - - mal
p
p
a gar - - - - - land, dis - - - - - - - - - - - - - -
6
12
p
Maid - ens, wil - low branch - - - - - - es,
p
Maid - ens, wil - low branch
p
Maid - - ens, wil - low
[p]
Maid - - ens, wil - low
- ens, wil - low branch - - - - es wear,
p
Maid - ens, wil - low branch - - es wear, Maid -
yew;
- - - - - - - - - - mal yew;
12

17

wil - low branch -

- es wear; Say she

branch - es wear;

branch - es wear; *cresc.* Say,

Maid - ens, wil - low *cresc.* branch -

- ens wil - low branch - es wear;

Maid - ens, wil - low branch - *cresc.*

Maid - ens, wil - low *cresc.* branch -

17

22

- es wear; *f* Say, say she di - *dim.* ed true,

di - *cresc.* ed true, *f* say she di - *dim.* ed true,

*f* Say she di - ed *dim.* true,

say she *f* di - ed true, *p* Her

- es wear; *f* Say she di - ed *dim.* true,

*cresc.* Say she di - ed *f* true, Say she *dim.* di - ed true,

- es wear; *f* Say she di - *dim.* ed true,

- es wear; *f* Say she di - ed true, *dim.*

22

28

p Her love cresc.

p Her love cresc.

p Her love cresc. was

love cresc.

Her love cresc.

cresc. Her love f

f Her love

f Her

28

34

f cresc. was dim. false, p but

cresc. was dim. false, p but she

f false, p Her love was false, but

was false,

was false, p Her love was false, but

was dim. false,

dim. p was false,

love was cresc. false,

34

39
she was firm.
was firm. p Up - on her bu - - ried
she was firm. p Up - - on her bu -
but she was firm.
she was firm. p Up - on her bu - - - -
p but she was firm.
p but she was firm. Up -
p but she was firm.
39
44
Up - - - - - - - - - on her bu - ried bo - - - dy
bo - - - - - - - - - - - - - - - - - dy lie
- - - - - - - ried bo - dy lie.
Up - on her bu - - - - - - - - - ried bo - dy
- - ried bo - dy lie, cresc. lie
Up - on cresc. her bo - dy lie.
- on cresc. her bu - ried bo - - -
Up - on cresc. her bu - ried bo - - - - - - - dy
44

49
lie light - ly, thou gen - - - - - - - - tle earth, thou
light - - - ly, Thou gen - - - tle earth, thou
cresc.
lie light - ly, thou gen - - - - - - - tle earth,
lie light - ly, thou gen - - - - - - - - - tle earth,
light - ly, thou gen - - - - - - - tle, gen - tle earth,
thou gen - - - - - - - tle earth, thou
- - dy lie, thou gen - - - - - - - - tle earth,
lie light - ly, thou gen - - - - - - - - tle earth,
49
54
p
gen - - - - - - - - - - - - - - - - - - tle earth.
p
gen - - - - - - - - - - - - - - - - - - tle earth.
p
thou gen - - - - - - - - tle, gen - - tle earth.
p
thou gen - - - - - - - - tle, gen - - tle earth.
p
thou gen - tle earth.
p
gen - - - - - - - tle earth, thou gen - - - tle earth.
p
thou gen - - tle, gen - - - - - - - tle earth.
p
thou gen - tle, gen - - - - - - - - tle earth.
54

# 20. THE LONG DAY CLOSES

Text
Henry F. Chorley

ARTHUR SULLIVAN

* The small notes in the Bass part are intended for use as *additional* notes, when the part-song is performed by a Chorus.

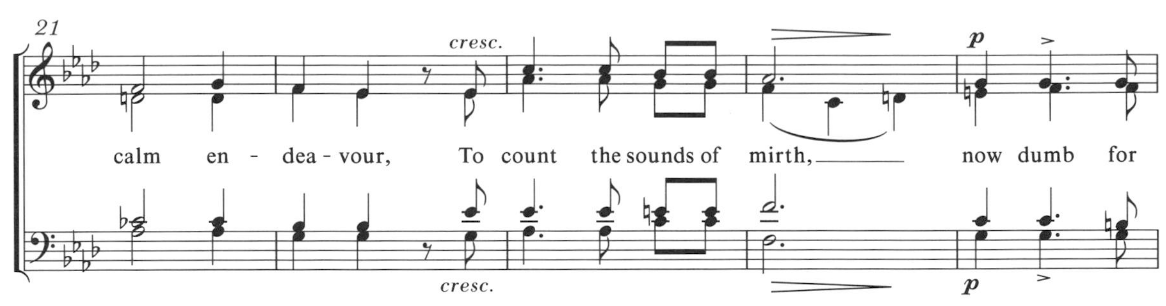
21
cresc.
p
calm en - dea - vour, To count the sounds of mirth, now dumb for
cresc.
p

26
f
ev - er. Heed not how hope be- lieves And fate dis - po - ses:
f

30
p
p
Sha- dow is round the eaves, The long day clo - ses. The
p
p
p
The light - ed win- dows

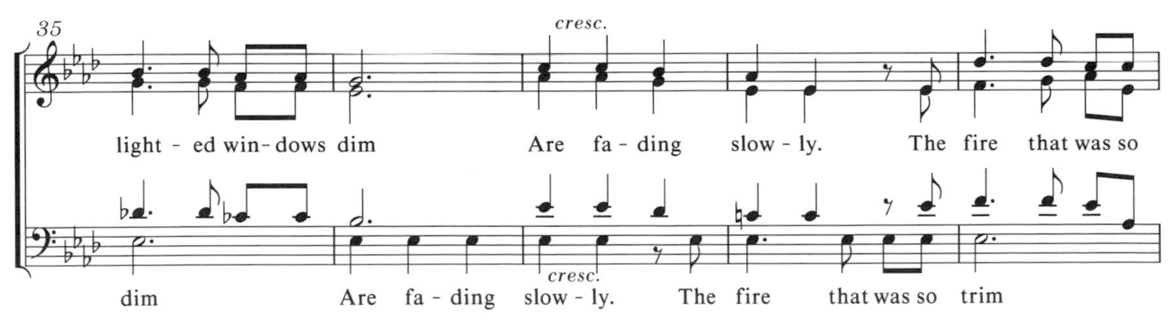
35
cresc.
light - ed win- dows dim Are fa - ding slow - ly. The fire that was so
dim Are fa - ding slow - ly. The fire that was so trim
cresc.

40
dim.
pp
trim Now quiv - ers lowly, quiv-ers low-ly. Go to the dream-less bed Where
Now quiv - ers
dim.
pp
45
cresc.
grief re - po - ses; Thy book of toil is read, The long day
cresc.
50
f
ff
clo-ses; Go to the dream-less bed Where grief re - po-ses; Thy
Go to the dream-less bed Where grief re - po-ses; Thy
f
ff
f Go to the dream-less bed Where grief re - po-ses; ff Thy
55
Go to the
dim.
p
thy book of toil is read, Go
book of toil is read,
Thy book of toil is read, Go
dim.
dim.
thy book of toil is read,
p
60
dream - less bed,
pp
to the dream - less bed, The long day clo - - - - ses.
pp

# 21. MADRIGAL

Text
Anon.

RICHARD RODNEY BENNETT
(b.1936)

**Poco allegro** (♩. = 80)

SOPRANO
*mf*
And can the phy - si - cian make sick men well?

ALTO
*mf*
And can the phy - si - cian make sick men well?

TENOR
*mf*
And can the phy - si - cian make

BASS
*mf*
And can the phy - si - cian make

**Poco allegro** (♩. = 80)

*Rehearsal accompaniment*

With - out li - ly, ger - man - der and
With - out li - ly, ger - man - der and
di - vine? With - out li - ly, ger -
di - vine? With - out li - ly, ger -
sops in wine, With sweet briar, and bon - fire and
sops in wine, With sweet briar, bon - fire,
- man - der and sops in wine, sweet briar, bon - fire,
- man - der and sops in wine, sweet briar,

11

*p* *pp*
straw-ber-ry wire and col-um-bine. With - in and out, in and out,

*mp* *p* *pp*
straw-ber-ry wire col-um-bine. With - in and out, in and out,

*mp* *p* *pp*
straw-ber-ry wire col-um-bine. With -

*mp* *p* *pp*
straw-ber-ry wire col-um-bine. With -

11

15

*p*
round as a ball. With hith - er and thith - er as straight as

*p*
round as a ball. With hith - er and thith - er as straight as

*p*
- in and out, in and out, round as a ball. With hith - er and

*p*
- in and out, in and out, round as a ball. With hith - er and

15

18
a line.
With
li - ly, ger - man - der and
a line.
With
li - ly, ger - man - der and
thith - er as straight as
a line.
With
li - - - ly, ger -
thith - er as straight as
a line.
With
li - - - ly, ger -
21
sops in wine,
With
sweet briar and bon - fire and
sops in wine,
With
sweet briar, bon - fire,
- man - der and sops in wine,
sweet briar, bon - fire,
- man - der and sops in wine,
sweet
briar,

24

*pp* *f subito*

straw-ber-ry wire and col-um-bine. When Sa-turn did live there

*pp* *f subito*

straw-ber-ry wire col-um-bine. When Sa-turn did live there

*pp* *f*

straw-ber-ry wire col-um-bine. there

*pp* *f*

straw-ber-ry wire col-um-bine. there

24

28

lived no poor. The king and the beg-gar on roots did

lived no poor. The king and the beg-gar on roots did

lived no poor. on roots did

lived no poor. on roots did

28

32
ff
f
dine, With li-ly, ger-man-der and sops in wine, With
dine, With li-ly, ger-man-der and sops in wine,
dine, With li - - ly, ger - man-der and sops in wine,
dine, With li - - ly, ger - man-der and sops in wine,
32
35
mf
li - ly, ger - man - der and sops in wine, With
li - ly, ger - man - der and sops in wine, With
li - - - - ly, ger - man - der and sops in wine,
li - - - - ly, ger - man - der and sops in wine,
35

37

mp p

sweet briar and bon - fire and straw-ber-ry wire and

mp

sweet briar, bon - - fire, straw-ber-ry wire,

mf mp

sweet briar, bon - - fire, straw-ber-ry wire,

mf mp

sweet briar, straw-ber-ry wire,

37

40

**poco rall.**

pp 2

col - um - bine, and col - um - bine.

p pp 2

col - um - bine, and col - um - bine.

p pp 2

col - um - bine, and col - um - bine.

p pp 2

col - um - bine, and col - um - bine.

40

**poco rall.**

2

2

# 22. THE MOON

Text
Charles Best

GEORGE DYSON
(1883-1964)

quasi f
in her sight, With full tide is rea - dy
quasi f
in his sight, With full tide is rea - dy
quasi f
in his sight, With full tide is rea - dy her to
quasi f
in his sight, With full tide is rea - dy
her to hon - our, is rea - dy her to
her to hon - - - - - our, is rea - dy her
hon - our, is rea - dy her to
her to hon - - - - - - our, her to
mf
hon - our. But when the sil - - ver wag - gon of the
mf
to hon - our. But when the sil - ver wag - gon of the
mf
hon - - - - - our. But when the wag - gon of the
mf
hon - our. But when the wag - gon of the

26
cresc.
f
moon Is mount - ed so high he can - - not fol - low, The
moon Is mount - - ed high he can - not fol - low, The
moon Is mount - ed so high he can - not fol - low, The
moon Is mount - ed so high he can - not fol - low, The
26
31
poco a poco dim.
sea calls home his cry - stal waves to moan
sea calls home his cry - stal waves to moan
sea calls home his cry - stal waves to moan
sea calls home his cry - - stal waves to moan
31
36
p
pp
And with low ebb doth man - i - fest his sor - - row.
And with low ebb doth man - i - fest his sor - - row.
And with low ebb doth man - i - fest his sor - - row.
And with low ebb doth man - i - fest his sor - - row.
36

43
mp
dolce
So you_ that are the sove-reign of my heart Have all my joys at - tend-ing on your
So you_ that are the sove-reign of my heart Have all my joys at - tend-ing on your
So you_ that are the sove-reign of my heart Have all my joys at - tend-ing on your
So you_ that are the sove-reign of my heart Have all my joys at - tend-ing on your
43
49
calando
will, So as you come_ and as you de-part, Joys ebb and
will,_ So_ as you come_ and as you de-part,_ Joys_ ebb and
will,_ So as you come_ and as_ you de-part,_ Joys ebb and
will, So as you come and de-part, Joys ebb and
49
55
p
pp
flow, Joys ebb and flow_ with-in_ my ten-der heart._
flow, Joys_ ebb and flow_ with-in_ my ten-der heart._
flow, Joys ebb and flow_ with-in my ten-der heart._
flow,_ Joys ebb and flow_ with-in my ten-der heart._
55

# 23. MUSIC, WHEN SOFT VOICES DIE

Text
Percy Bysshe Shelley

GEOFFREY BUSH
(1920 - 1998)

7

*cresc.*

Live with-in the sense they quick - en, with - in the sense they

*cresc.*

Live in sense they quick - en, the sense they

sick - en, Live with-in the sense they quick - en, they

*cresc.*

Live with-in the sense they quick - en, the sense they

7

10

*pp teneramente*

quick-en. Rose leaves, when the rose is dead, Are heap'd for a be -

*pp teneramente*

quick-en. Rose leaves, when the rose is dead, Are for

*pp teneramente* *espressivo*

quick-en. Rose leaves, when the rose is dead,

*pp teneramente*

quick-en. Rose leaves, when the rose is dead, Are for be - lov-ed's

10

13
dim.
- lov - ed's bed; And so thy thoughts, when thou art gone, Love it -
be- lov- ed's bed; And so thy thoughts, when thou art gone, thou art
cresc.
Are for a bed; And so thy thoughts when thou art gone, thou art
bed; And so thy thoughts, when thou art
16
poco rit.
a tempo
p
- self shall slum - - ber, slum - ber on,
mp
Love shall slum - ber
gone,
(Mu - sic, when soft voi - ces die,)
gone,
(Mu - sic, when soft voi - ces die,)
gone,
(Mu - sic, when soft voi - ces die,)

19

on, shall slum-ber on, Love it - self shall

(Mu-sic, when soft voi-ces die,) Love shall slum - ber

(Mu-sic, when soft voi-ces die,) Love shall slum-ber

(Mu-sic, when soft voi-ces die,) Love shall slum - ber

22

poco rit. al fine

slum-ber, slum-ber, Love shall slum-ber on.

on, slum - - - - - ber on.

on, shall slum - - ber on.

on, slum - - - - - ber on.

poco rit. al fine

# 24. MY DELIGHT AND THY DELIGHT

Text
Robert Bridges

C. HUBERT H. PARRY
(1848 - 1918)

allargando
Twi-ning to a tongue of fire, Leap-ing live, and laugh-ing higher, Thro' the
Twi - - ning to a tongue of fire, Leap-ing live, and laugh-ing higher, Thro' the
tranquillo
e-ver-last-ing strife, In the mys - - - - te-ry of life.

17
animato
animando
f
cresc.
p
Love, from whom the world be-gun, Hath the se - - cret of the sun. Love can
Love, from whom the world be-gun, Hath the se - - cret of the sun. Love can
Love, from whom the world be-gun, Hath the se - - cret of the sun. Love
Love, from whom the world be-gun, Hath the se - - cret of the sun. Love can
21
tell, and love a-lone, Whence the mil - lion stars were strewn, Why each
tell, and love a-lone, Whence the mil - lion stars were strewn, Why each
can tell, and love a-lone, Whence the mil-lion stars were strewn, Why
tell, and love a-lone, Whence the mil - lion stars were strewn, Why each

25
a - tom knows its own, How in spite of woe and death Gay is
a - tom knows its own, How in spite of woe and death Gay is
each a - tom knows its own, How in spite of woe and death Gay is
a - tom knows its own, How in spite of woe and death Gay is
25
meno mosso
Tempo primo
29
p dolce legato
life, and sweet is breath. This he taught us, this we knew, Hap- py in his
life, and sweet is breath. This he taught us, this we knew, Hap- py in his
life, and sweet is breath. This he taught us, this we knew, Hap- py in his
life, and sweet is breath. This he taught us, this we knew, Hap- py in his
meno mosso
Tempo primo
29

35
poco animando
cresc. molto
mf
sci- ence true, Hand to hand as we stood, 'Neath the sha- dows of the wood, Heart to
sci- ence true, Hand to hand as we stood, 'Neath the sha - dows of the wood, Heart to
sci- ence true, Hand to hand as we stood, 'Neath the sha - dows of the wood, Heart to
sci- ence true, Hand to hand as we stood, 'Neath the sha - dows of the wood, Heart to
35
poco animando
40
heart as we lay In the dawn-ing of the day, in the dawn - -
heart as we lay In the dawn - ing of the day, in the dawn - -
heart as we lay In the dawn-ing of the day, in the dawn - -
heart as we lay In the dawn - ing of the day, in the dawn - -
40

45

*mf* *pp*

- ing of the day, Heart to heart as we lay, In the dawn - -

*mf* *pp*

- ing of the day, Heart to heart as we lay, In the dawn - -

*mf* *pp*

- ing of the day, Heart to heart as we lay, In the dawn - -

*mf* *pp*

- ing of the day, Heart to heart as we lay, In the dawn - -

45

50

*p* *sempre dim.* **rit.**

- - - - - - ing, the dawn - - - - ing of the day.

*sempre dim.*

- - - - - - ing, the dawn - - - - - - - - - - - ing of the day.

*sempre dim.*

- - - - - - ing the dawn - - - - - - - - - - - ing of the day.

*sempre dim.* div.

- - - - - - ing, the dawn - - - - - ing of the day.

50

**rit.**

# 25. MY SOUL WOULD DRINK THOSE ECHOES

Text
Lord Byron

ALEXANDER MACKENZIE
(1847 - 1935)

Più mosso (♩= 76)
molto espress.
dim.
poco rit.
p
A liv - - - - ing
A liv - - - - ing
stentando
that I were The view - less spi - rit of a love - - - - ly sound, A
p molto dim.
unis.
that I were The view - less spi - rit of a love - - - - ly sound, A
poco rit.
Più mosso (♩= 76)
poco stringendo
a breath - ing, breath - - -
mp
div.
voice, a liv - - - ing voice, a breath - ing har - mo - ny, a
a breath - ing har - mo - ny, a
unis.
div.
voice, a liv - - - ing voice, a breath - ing, breath - - -
a breath - ing, breath - - -
liv - ing voice, a voice, a breath - ing har - mo - ny, a
a breath - ing har - mo - ny, a
liv - ing voice, a voice, a breath - ing har - mo - ny, a
poco stringendo

allargando
- - - ing
17
unis.
tranquillo
corta
breath - ing har - mo - ny, A bo - di - less en - joy - ment,
breath - ing har - mo - ny, A bo - di - less, a
- - - ing har - mo - ny, A bo - di - less en - joy - ment,
- - - ing har - mo - ny, A
breath - ing har - mo - ny, A bo - di - less, a bo - di - less en - joy - ment,
breath - ing har - mo - ny, A bo - di - less en - joy - ment,
17
allargando
tranquillo
22
espress.
stringendo
born and dy - ing, born and dy - ing With the blest
born and dy - ing, born and dy - ing With the blest
born, dy - ing, born, dy - ing With the blest
born and dy - ing, born and dy - ing With the blest
22
stringendo

27
allargando
mf
f
mp
tone that made me, with the blest tone that made me. A
tone that made me, with the blest tone that made me. A
div.
tone that made me, with the blest tone that made me.
tone that made me, tone that
tone, with the blest tone that made me, A
27
allargando
a tempo
con espress.
32
poco stringendo
div.
p
liv - - ing voice, a liv - - ing voice, a breath - ing,
liv - - ing voice, a liv - - ing voice, a breath - ing,
unis.
div.
A liv - - ing voice, a voice, a breath - ing,
breath - ing,
liv - - ing voice, a liv - - ing voice, a breath - ing
32
a tempo
poco stringendo

breath - - - - - - - - - ing
37
unis.
allargando
tranquillo
breath - - ing, breath - - ing har - mo - ny. A
breath - - ing, breath - - ing har - mo - ny, A bo - di - less, a
breath - - - - - - - - - ing har - mo - ny, A
breath - - - - - - - - - ing har - mo - ny, A
breath - - ing, breath - ing har - mo - ny, A bo - di - less, a
breath - - ing, breath - ing
har - mo - ny, a breath - ing har - mo - ny, A
37
allargando
tranquillo
41
corta
espress.
bo - di - less en - joy - ment, born and dy - ing, born and dy - ing
corta
espress.
bo - di - less en - joy - ment, born and dy - ing, born and dy - ing
unis.
corta
espress.
bo - di - less en - joy - ment, born, dy - ing, born dy - ing
corta
espress.
bo - di - less en - joy - ment, born and dy - ing, born and dy - ing
41
corta

47

stringendo — tranquillo — molto dim.

mp mf mp

With the blest tone that made me,— with the blest tone that

unis. div. unis.

With the blest tone— that— made me,— with the blest tone that

tone— that—

div.

With the blest tone— that made me,— with the blest tone that

tone— that— made me,—

With the blest— tone— with the blest tone that

47

stringendo — tranquillo

52

rit. — lunga — Tempo primo Lento

pp p

made me.— My soul would drink those e - choes-—

made me.— My soul would drink those e - choes-—

made me.— My soul would drink those

made me.— My soul would drink those

52

rit. — Tempo primo Lento

allargandosi molto
57
div.
unis.
stentando
cresc.
Oh, that I were The view - less spi-rit of a love - ly
Oh, that I were The view - less spi - rit of a love - ly, love - ly
spi-rit
e-choes- Oh, that I were The view - less spi - rit of a love - ly
spi - rit
e-choes- Oh, that I were The view-less, view - less spi-rit of a love - ly
allargandosi molto
57
62
sound.
molto dim.
rit.
morendo, molto dim.
lunga
sound, of a love - ly sound.
lunga
estinto
sound.
morendo
sound, of a love - ly sound, of a love - ly sound.
sound.
sound, of a love - ly sound.
sound, of a love - ly sound.
62
rit.
lunga

*Composed and Dedicated to Joseph Gwilt*

# 26. O SING UNTO MY ROUNDELAY

Text
Thomas Chatterton

SAMUEL WESLEY
(1766-1837)
Edited by A.H. Mann

[p]
[rall.]
[faster]
Loud
-lay, Drop the briny tear with me, O sing unto my roundelay, unto my roundelay;
-lay, O drop the briny tear with me, O sing unto my roundelay, unto my roundelay; Drop the briny tear with me;
-lay, O sing, O sing unto my roundelay, my roundelay; Drop the briny tear with me;
Drop the briny tear with me, with me, O sing un to my roundelay;
O sing unto my roundelay; Drop the briny tear with me;
[slightly slower]
[rall.]
Soft.

Loud
Dance no more, dance no more on ho - li - day, dance no more on
Dance no more, dance no more on ho - li - day, dance no more on
Dance no more, dance no more on ho - li - day, dance no more on
Dance no more, dance no more on ho - li - day, dance no more on
Dance no more on ho - li - day, dance no more on
[f]
Piano and smoothly
ho - li - day; Like a run - ning riv - er
ho - li - day; Like a run - ning riv - er be, a run - ning, run - ning riv - er
ho - li - day;
ho - li - day; Like a run - ning, run - ning riv - er
ho - li - day;
* autograph has
on
† autograph has
ho - li - day,

25

[ff]

be, a run - ning riv - er, like a run - ning riv - - - - er be;

be, a run - ning riv - er, a run - ning riv - er be;

*Piano and smoothly*

Like a run - ning riv - er be, like a run-ning riv - - - - er be;

be, like a run - ning riv - - - - er be;

*Piano and smoothly*

Like a run - ning riv - er be, a run - ning riv - er be;

25

29

*Soft.* [dim.]

My love is dead, Gone to his death - - bed, All un -

*Soft.* [dim.]

My love is dead, Gone to his death - - bed, All un -

*Soft.* [dim.]

My love is dead, Gone to his death - - bed,

*Soft.*

My love is dead, All un -

*Soft.* [dim.]

Gone to his death - - bed,

29

* D in autograph

* Two quavers, G,D, in autograph

† autograph has

sing un - to my roun - de -

42
[rall.]
Soft
- lay; Drop the briny tear with me; My love is dead, Gone
- lay; O drop the bri - ny tear with me; My love is dead, Gone,
- lay; My love is dead, Gone,
- lay; Drop the bri - ny tear with me;
- lay;
47
[dim.]
to his death - bed, All un - der the wil - low tree, all un - der the wil - low
gone to his death - bed, All un - der the wil - low tree, all un - der the wil - low
gone to his death - bed, All un - der the wil - low
All un - der the wil - low tree, all un - der the wil - low
All un - der the wil - low
* autograph has Drop
† autograph has un - der the

52
Loud
Soft
tree, My love, my love is dead, Gone to his death - bed, All un-der the wil-low
tree, My love, my love is dead, Gone to his death - bed, All un-der the wil-low
tree, My love is dead, Gone to his death - bed, Un-der the wil - low
tree, My love is dead, Gone to his death - bed, Un-der the wil-low
tree, My love is dead, Gone to his death - bed,
52
58
[pp]
tree, all un-der the wil - - - - - - low tree, My love is
tree, all un-der the wil - - - - - - low tree, My love is
tree, all un - der the wil - - low tree, My love is
tree, My love is dead,
all un-der the wil - low tree, My love is dead,
58

63
dead, Gone to his death - bed, All un - der the wil - low tree, all
dead, Gone, gone to his death - - bed, All un - der the wil - low tree, all
dead, Gone, gone to his death - bed,
All un - der the wil - low tree, all
63
68
Loud
un - der the wil - low tree, My love, my love is dead, Gone to his death -
un - der the wil - low tree. My love, my love is dead, Gone to his death -
My love is dead, Gone to his death -
un - der the wil - low tree, My love is dead, Gone to his death -
My love is dead, Gone to his death -
68

73
[p]
- bed, Un - der the wil - low, wil - low_ tree, un - der the wil - low, wil - low_
[p]
- bed, Un - der the wil - low, wil - low_ tree, un - der the wil - low, wil - low_
[p]
- bed, Un - der, un - der the wil - low, wil - low_ tree, un - der the wil - low,
[p]
- bed, All un - der the wil - low tree, all un - der the wil - low
- bed,
73
77
tree, un - der the wil - low, the wil - low tree, un - der the
[pp]
tree, un - der the wil - low, the wil - low tree, un - der the
[pp]
wil - low_ tree, the_ wil - low tree, all_ un - der,
[pp]
tree, un - der the wil - low tree, un -
[pp]
All un - der the wil - low tree,
77

81
Loud
wil - low, wil - low_ tree, un - der the wil - low, wil - low_ tree, un - der the
Loud
wil - low, wil - low tree,___ un - - - - der the
Loud
un - der the wil - low tree, the_ wil - - - - - - low tree,___ un - -
Loud
- der the wil - low tree, all un - der the wil - low tree, un - -
81
85
[cresc. and slower to end]
wil - low tree, the wil - - - low tree.
[cresc. and slower to end]
wil - - - - - - - low tree, the wil - - low tree.
[cresc. and slower to end]
- der the wil - - - - - low tree, the wil - - - - - low tree.___
[cresc. and slower to end]
- der the wil - low tree, all un - der the wil - - low tree.___
Loud [cresc. and slower to end]
all un - der the wil - low tree.
85
cresc. and slower to end
*autograph has
- der the

# 27. ORPHEUS, WITH HIS LUTE

( No. 1 of *Shakspeare Songs*)

Text
William Shakespeare

GEORGE MACFARREN
(1813-1887)

11
f dim.
he did sing, made trees and moun-tains Bow them-selves when he did
f dim.
he did sing, made moun-tains Bow when he did
f dim.
he did sing, made trees and moun-tains Bow them-selves when he did
f dim.
he did sing, made trees Bow when he did
p
11
16
f
sing; To his mu-sic plants and flow-ers, plants and flow-ers E-ver sprung,
sing; To his mu-sic plants and flow-ers, plants and flow-ers E-ver sprung, as
sing; To his mu-sic plants and flow-ers, plants and flow-ers E-ver sprung,
sing; To his mu-sic plants and flow-ers, plants and flow-ers E-ver sprung,
16
21
p
as sun and show-ers There had made a last-ing spring; E-ve-ry thing that
sun and show-ers There had made a last-ing spring; E-ve-ry thing that
as sun and show-ers There had made a last-ing spring; E-ve-ry thing that
There had made a last-ing spring;
21

26
heard him play, E - ve-ry thing that heard him play, E - ven the bil - lows
heard him play, E - ve-ry thing that heard him play,
heard him play, E - ve-ry thing that heard him play, E - ven the bil - lows
E - ve-ry thing that heard him play, E - ven the
pp
30
of the sea, E - ven the bil - lows of the sea Hung their heads and then lay by,
E - ven the bil - lows of the sea Hung their heads and then lay by,
of the sea, E - ven the bil - lows Hung their heads and then lay by,
bil - lows of the sea Hung their heads and then lay by,
sf p
35
dim.
Hung their heads and then lay by. In sweet mu - sic, In sweet mu - sic, In sweet
pp
cresc.

40
dim.
poco rit.
a tempo
mu - sic is such art, In sweet music is such
mu - sic is such art, In sweet mu - sic is such
mu - sic is such art, In sweet mu - - - - sic, In sweet mu - sic is such
mu - sic is such art, In sweet mu - sic is such
46
art, In mu - sic is such art, Kill - ing care and grief of heart, and grief of
art, In mu - sic is such art, Kill - ing care and grief of heart, and grief
art, In mu - sic is such art, Kill - ing care and grief of heart, and grief
art, In mu - sic is such art, Fall a-
52
pp cresc.
dim.
heart. Fall a - sleep, fall a - sleep, or, hear - ing, die, or, hear - ing,
of heart. Fall a - sleep, fall a - sleep, or, hear - ing, die, or, hear - ing,
of heart. Fall a - sleep, fall a - sleep, or, hear - ing, die, or, hear - ing,
- sleep, Fall a - sleep, or, hear - ing, die, or,

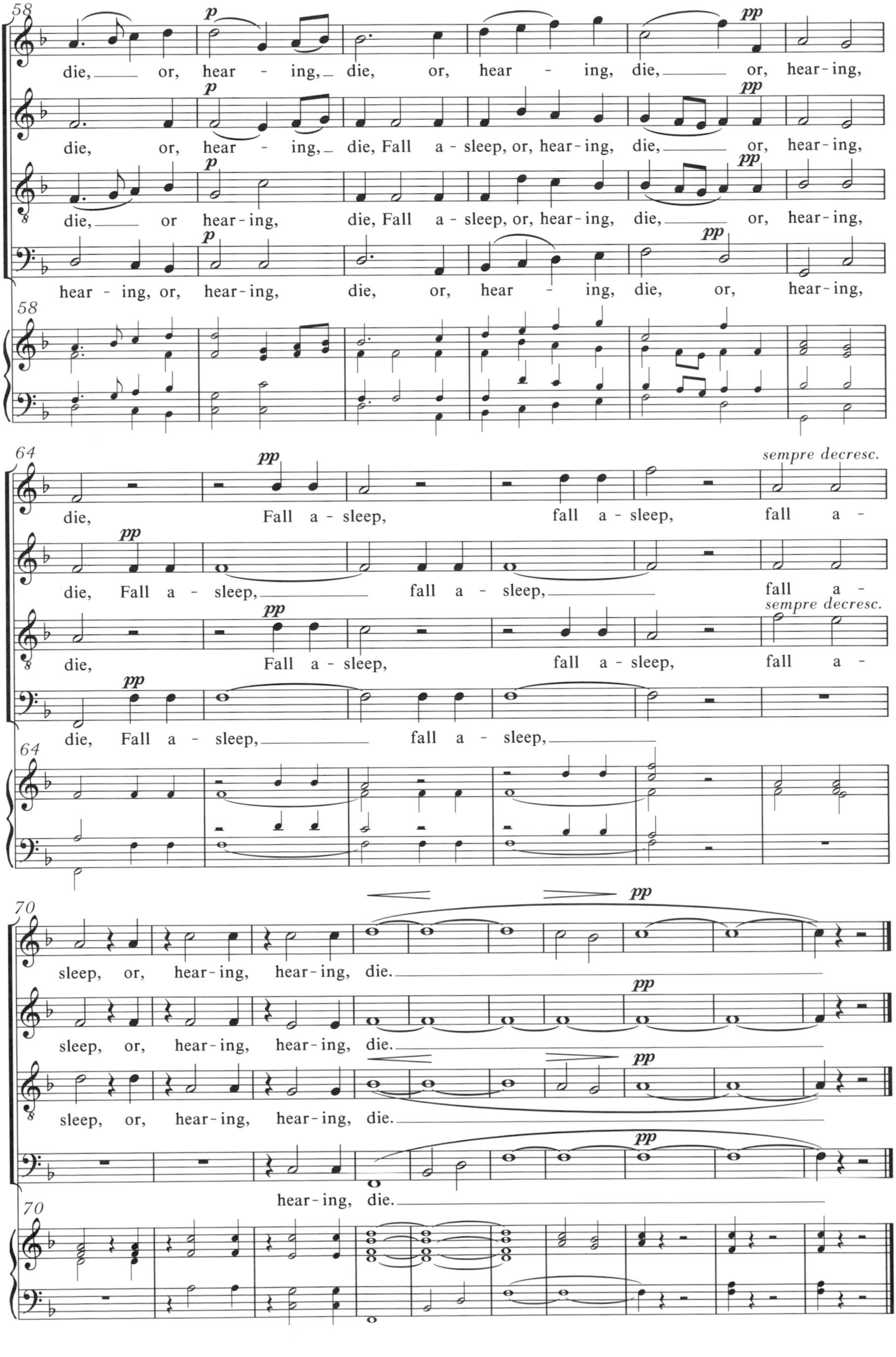

58
p
pp
die, or, hear - ing, die, or, hear - ing, die, or, hear-ing,
die, or, hear - ing, die, Fall a-sleep, or, hear-ing, die, or, hear-ing,
die, or hear-ing, die, Fall a-sleep, or, hear-ing, die, or, hear-ing,
hear-ing, or, hear-ing, die, or, hear - ing, die, or, hear-ing,
64
sempre decresc.
die, Fall a-sleep, fall a-sleep, fall a -
die, Fall a - sleep, fall a - sleep, fall a -
die, Fall a-sleep, fall a-sleep, fall a -
die, Fall a - sleep, fall a - sleep,
70
sleep, or, hear-ing, hear-ing, die.
sleep, or, hear-ing, hear-ing, die.
sleep, or, hear-ing, hear-ing, die.
hear-ing, die.

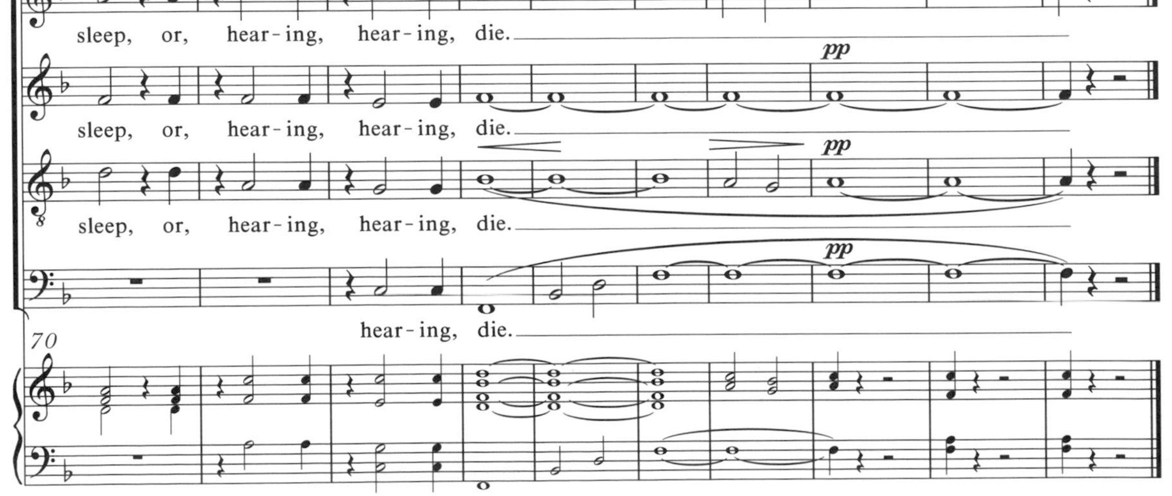

# 28. THE PRINCE OF SLEEP

Words by
Walter de la Mare

EDWARD ELGAR
(1857-1934)

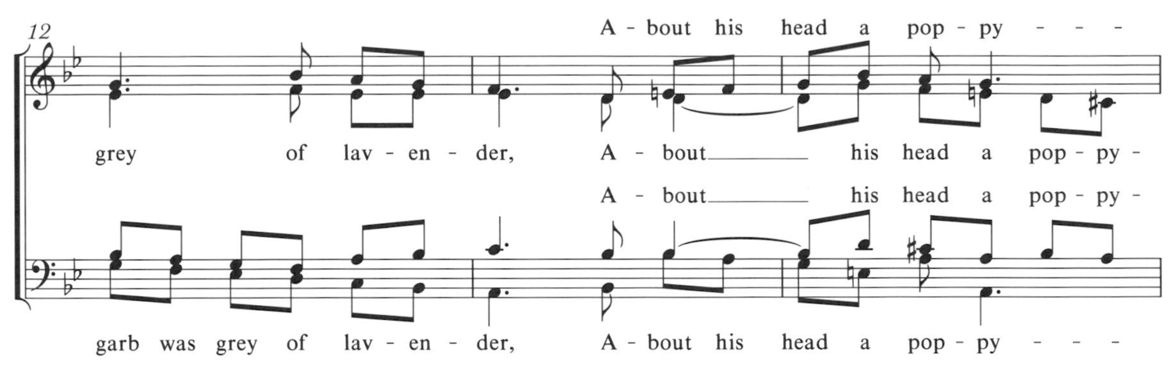
12
A - bout his head a pop - py - - -
grey of lav - en - der, A - bout his head a pop - py -
A - bout his head a pop - py -
garb was grey of lav - en - der, A - bout his head a pop - py - - -

15
where The air was sweet -
- wreath Burned like dim coals, and ev - 'ry - where The air was
where The air was sweet -
where The air was

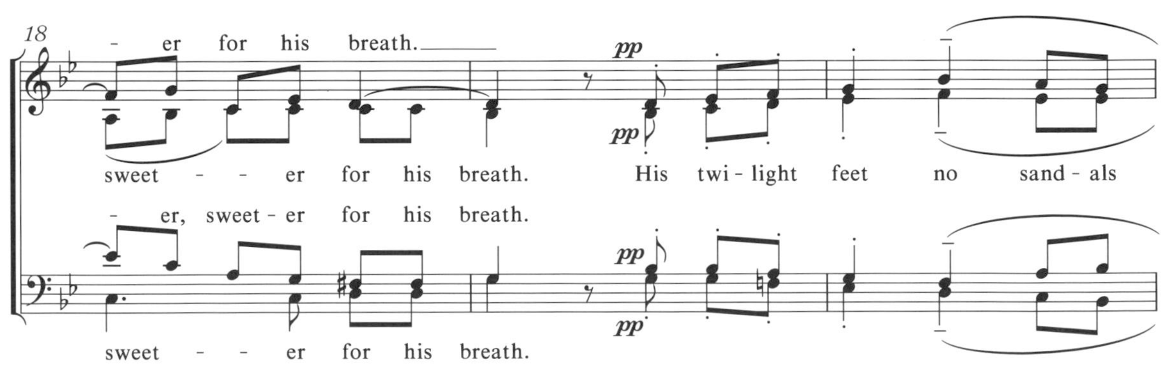
18
- er for his breath.
pp
pp
sweet - - er for his breath. His twi - light feet no sand - als
- er, sweet - er for his breath.
pp
pp
sweet - - er for his breath.

21
sosten.
sosten.
wore, His eyes shone faint in their own flame, Fair moths that
sosten.
sosten.

24
gloomed his steps be - fore Seemed let - ters of his love - ly name.
pp
Poco più mosso (♩= 76)
dolce e legato
28
His house is in the moun - tain ways, A phan - tom
33
mf cantabile
house of mis - - ty walls, Whose gold - en flocks at
pp
38
moon with muff - led
eve - ning graze, And witch the moon with
moon, and witch the
42
calls.
muff - led calls. Up - well - ing from his sha - dow - y
moon with muff - led calls. From his sha - dow - y

47
cresc.
springs Sweet wa - ters shake a tremb - ling sound, There
p
cresc.
52
flit the hoot - owl's si - lent wings, There hath his
56
web the silk - worm wound
rit.
a tempo (♩= 58)
dim.
web, his web the silk - worm wound. Dark in his
web, his web, his web the silk - worm wound. Dark
dim.
web, his web the silk - worm wound. Dark
61
pools clear vis - ions lurk,
in his pools clear vis - ions lurk,
And ros - y, as with morn - ing
64
buds, A - long his dales of broom and birk* Dreams
pp

*birk = birch

67
rit.
Come prima, più lento (♩= 60)
ppp
haunt his sol - - - - i - ta - ry woods.
I
ppp
ppp
woods.
70
met at eve the Prince of Sleep, His was a still and
div.
unis.
div.
unis.
73
3
love - ly face; He wan - der'd through a val - ley steep,
S I
rit. al fine
76
dolce ten.
pp
div.
div.
pp
S II
Love - - - - ly in a lone - ly place, in a lone - - - ly place.
pp
Love - - - - ly in a lone - - - - ly, a lone - - - ly place.
Love-ly, love - ly in a lone - ly place, in a lone - - - ly place.
pp
dolce ten.
div.
Love - - - - ly

*For Stephen, on his 70th Birthday*

# 29. PROUD SONGSTERS

Text
Thomas Hardy

JOHN McCABE
(b.1939)

7
cresc.
p
mf
the finch-es whis-tle in ones and pairs, And
in ones and pairs, And
the finch-es whis-tle in ones and pairs, And
in ones and pairs, And
10
f
as it gets dark loud night-in-gales In bush-es Pipe,
as it gets dark loud night-in-gales In bush-es Pipe,
as it gets dark loud night-in-gales In bush-es Pipe,
as it gets dark loud night-in-gales In bush-es Pipe,

13
dim.
p
Pipe, as they
can when A - pril wears, As if all Time
16
cresc.
f
div.

were theirs.
These are
were theirs.
These are brand-new birds
were theirs.
These are
unis.
were theirs.
These are brand-new birds
brand-new birds
of twelve-months grow
of twelve-months grow
brand-new birds
of twelve-months grow
of twelve-months grow
cresc.

27
p
mp
p
mf
p
ing, Which a year a - go, or less than twain,
31
f
p
cresc.
No fin - ches were, nor night - in - gales, Nor thrush - - - -

dim.
f
- es, But on - ly par - - - - - - - ti - cles of
div.
unis.
of
S. SOLO
p
grain, And earth, and air, and rain.
S.
pp
grain.
A. SOLO
T. SOLO
B. SOLO
A.
T.
B.

# 30. A SHEPHERD'S CAROL

Text
W.H. Auden

BENJAMIN BRITTEN
(1913 - 1976)

pinkie = finger horse opera = Western

CHORUS
Tempo I
S.
A.
T.
B.
pp
ten.
O lift your lit - - tle pin - kie, and
touch the win - ter sky.
pp
più f
Love's all o - ver the
mountains where the beau - ti - ful go to die.
dim.
TENOR SOLO
Allegretto
p con eleganza
2. If I were a Va - len - tine, and For - tune were a - broad, I'd
espress.
pp leggiero
hyp - no - tise that ice - berg till she kissed me of her own ac - cord - O.
CHORUS
Tempo I
O lift your lit - - tle pin - kie, and

31
touch the win - ter sky.
Love's all o - ver the
pp
più f
34
moun - tains where the beau - ti - ful go to die.
ten.
dim.
pp
ALTO SOLO
Vivace
ff pesante e giocoso
37
3. If I'd stacked up the vel - vet and my crook - ed rib were dead, I'd be
41
breed - ing white ca - na - ries and eat - ing crack - ers in bed - O.
rall.
Tempo I
S.
A.
T.
B.
mp
45
O lift your lit - - tle pin - kie, and
ten.
47
touch the win - ter sky.
Love's all o - ver the
mp
più f

49
ten.
dim.
mp
moun-tains where the beau-ti-ful go to die.
SOPRANO SOLO
Andante mesto
pp
52
4. But my cuffs are soiled and fray-ing. The kit-chen clock is
con espanione
55
pp
slow, and o-ver the Blue Wa-ters the grass grew long a-go.
Tempo I
S.
A.
ppp
60
O lift your lit-tle pin-kie, and
T.
B.
ppp
ten.
62
pp
f
touch the win-ter sky. Love's all o-ver the
molto rall.
ten.
dim.
ppp
moun-tains where the beau-ti-ful go to die.

# 31. SIGH NO MORE, LADIES

( No.5 of *Songs of Springtime*)

Text
William Shakespeare

E.J. MOERAN
(1894-1950)

8
mf
mp
never: Then sigh not so, but let them go, And be you blithe and bonny, Con-
never: Then sigh not so, but let them go, And be you blithe and bonny, Con-
never: Then sigh not so, but let them go, And be you blithe and bonny, Con-
never: Then sigh not so, but let them go, And be you blithe and bonny, Con-
8
13
poco accel.
poco animato
mf
f
div.
unis.
-verting all your sounds of woe Into Hey nonny, Hey nonny, Hey nonny,
-verting all your sounds of woe Into Hey nonny, Hey nonny, Hey nonny,
-verting all your sounds of woe Into Hey nonny, Hey nonny, Hey nonny,
-verting all your sounds of woe Into Hey nonny, Hey nonny, Hey nonny,
13
poco accel.
poco animato

18
mp
Hey non - ny, non - ny, non-ny non-ny non - ny,
mp
Hey non - ny, non - ny, non-ny non-ny non - ny,
mp
Hey non - ny, Hey non - ny, Hey non - ny non - ny,
mp
mp
Hey non - ny, Hey, Hey non - ny, Hey non - ny,
18
23
mf
p
p
non-ny non-ny non - ny, non-ny non-ny
mf
p
p
non-ny non-ny non - ny, non-ny non-ny
mf
p
non - ny, Hey non - ny, Hey non - ny, Hey non - ny non - ny,
mf
p
Hey non - ny, Hey non - ny, Hey non - ny, Hey non - ny non - ny,
23

28
poco rall.
Tempo I
mp
non-ny.
Sing no more dit-ties, sing no moe Of
non-ny.
Sing no more dit-ties, sing no moe Of
pp
Hey, Hey non-ny non-ny.
Sing no more dit-ties, sing no moe Of
Hey, Hey non-ny non-ny.
Sing no more dit-ties, sing no moe Of
34
mf
mp
p
dumps so dull and heav-y; The fraud of men was ev-er so, Since
dumps so dull and heav-y; The fraud of men was ev-er so, Since
dumps so dull and heav-y; The fraud of men was ev-er so, Since
dumps so dull and heav-y; The fraud of men was ev-er so, Since

38
sum-mer first was leav-y: Then sigh not so, but let them go, And
poco accel.
42
be you blithe and bon-ny, Con-vert-ing all your sounds of woe In-to
p
mf
mp

poco animato
Hey, non-ny, Hey non-ny, Hey non-ny, Hey non-ny, non-ny, non-ny non-ny
div. unis.
Hey, non-ny, Hey non-ny, Hey non-ny, Hey non-ny, non-ny, non-ny non-ny
Hey, non-ny, Hey non-ny, Hey non-ny, Hey non-ny, Hey non-ny, Hey non - ny
Hey, non-ny, Hey non-ny, Hey non-ny, Hey non-ny, Hey,
poco animato
non-ny, non-ny non-ny non-ny,
non-ny, non-ny non-ny non-ny,
non-ny, non-ny, Hey non - ny, Hey non-ny, Hey non-ny
Hey, non-ny, Hey non-ny, Hey non-ny, Hey non - ny, Hey, non-ny, Hey non-ny,

58

non-ny non-ny non-ny, non-ny non-ny non-ny,

non-ny non-ny non-ny, non-ny non-ny non-ny,

non-ny, Hey, Hey non-ny non-ny, Hey, Hey non-ny non-ny,

non-ny, Hey, Hey non-ny non-ny, Hey, Hey non-ny non-ny,

65

non-ny non-ny non-ny.

non-ny non-ny non-ny.

Hey, Hey non-ny, Hey non - ny, Hey non-ny, Hey non-ny non-ny.

Hey, Hey non-ny, Hey non - ny, Hey non-ny, Hey non-ny non-ny.

# 32. SLEEP! THE BIRD IS IN ITS NEST

10
in its nest; Sleep! the bee is hush'd in rest; Sleep! rock'd on thy moth - er's breast!
in its nest; Sleep! the bee is hush'd in rest; Sleep! rock'd on thy moth - er's breast!
- by, lul - la - by, lul - la - by, rock'd on thy moth - er's breast!
in its nest; Sleep! the bee is hush'd in rest; Sleep! rock'd on thy moth-er's breast!
- by, lul - la - by, lul - la - by,
10
15
cresc.
pp
Lul - la, lul - la - by; To thy moth - er's fond heart press'd, Lul - la, lul - la-
Lul - la, lul - la - by; To thy moth - er's fond heart press'd,
Lul - la, lul - la - by; To thy moth - er's fond heart press'd, Lul - la, lul - la-
Lul - la, lul - la - by; To thy moth - er's fond heart press'd, Lul - la, lul - la-
Lul - la, lul - la - by; To thy moth - er's fond heart press'd, Lul - la, lul - la-
15

20
- by, lul - la, lul - la - by, lul - la, lul - la - by.
pp
Lul - la, lul - la - by, lul - la, lul - la - by, lul - la - by.
- by, O lul - la - by, lul - la - by, O lul - la - by, lul - la - by.
- by, O lul - la - by, lul - la - by, lul - la, lul - la - by.
div.
- by, lul - la - by, O lul - la - by, lul - la - by.
20
27
mp
cresc.
dim.
Sleep! the wan - ing day - light dies; Sleep! the stars dream in the skies; Dai - sies long have
Sleep! the wan - ing day - light dies; Sleep! the stars dream in the skies; Dai - sies long have
Lul - la - by, lul - la - by, lul - la - by, Dai-sies long have
Sleep! the wan - ing day - light dies; Sleep! the stars dream in the skies; Dai - sies long have
unis.
Lul - la - by, lul - la - by, lul - la -
27

32
pp
closed their eyes; Lul - la, lul - la - by, Sleep! the wan - ing day - light dies;
closed their eyes; Lul - la, lul - la - by, Sleep! the wan - ing day - light dies;
closed their eyes; Lul - la, lul - la - by, lul - la - - by,
closed their eyes; Lul - la, lul - la - by, Sleep! the wan - ing day - light dies;
- by, lul - la - by, lul - la - - by,
32
37
Sleep! the stars dream in the skies; Dai - sies long have closed their eyes; Lul - la, lul - la-
Sleep! the stars dream in the skies; Dai - sies long have closed their eyes; Lul - la, lul - la-
lul - la - by, lul - la - by. Dai-sies long have closed their eyes; Lul - la, lul - la-
Sleep! the stars dream in the skies; Dai - sies long have closed their eyes; Lul - la, lul - la-
lul - la - by, lul - - la - by, lul - la, lul - la-
37

42
cresc.
pp
- by. Calm, how calm on all things lies! Lul - la, lul - la - by, lul - la, lul - la-
cresc.
pp
- by. Calm, how calm on all things lies! Lul - la, lul - la - by,
cresc.
pp
- by. Calm, how calm on all things lies! Lul - la, lul - la - by, O lul - la - by, lul - la-
cresc.
pp
- by. Calm, how calm on all things lies! Lul - la, lul - la - by, O lul - la - by, lul - la-
cresc.
pp
- by. Calm, how calm on all things lies! Lul - la, lul - la - by, lul - la -
42
48
mp
cresc.
- by, lul - la, lul - la - by. Sleep, then, sleep! my heart's de - light;
mp
cresc.
lul - la, lul - la - by, lul - la - by. Sleep, then, sleep! my heart's de - light;
mp
- by, O lul - la - by, lul - la - by. Lul - la - by,
mp
cresc.
- by, lul - la, lul - la - by, Sleep, then, sleep! my heart's de - light;
div.
unis.
mp
- by, O lul - la - by, lul - la - by. Lul - la - by,
48

55

*dim.*

Sleep! and thro' the dark-some night Round thy bed God's an - gels bright, Lul-la, lul-la - by,

*dim.*

Sleep! and thro' the dark-some night Round thy bed God's an - gels bright, Lul-la, lul-la - by,

*dim.*

lul - la - by, lul - la-by, Round thy bed God's an - gels bright, Lul-la, lul-la-by,

*dim.*

Sleep! and thro' the dark-some night Round thy bed God's an - gels bright, Lul-la, lul-la - by,

*dim.*

lul - la - by, lul - la - by, lul - la - by,

55

61

*pp*

Sleep, then sleep! my heart's de-light; Sleep! and thro' the dark-some night Round thy bed God's

*pp*

Sleep, then sleep! my heart's de-light; Sleep! and thro' the dark-some night Round thy bed God's

*pp*

Lul - la - by, lul - la - by, lul - la - by, Round thy bed God's

*pp*

Sleep, then sleep! my heart's de-light; Sleep! and thro' the dark-some night Round thy bed God's

*pp*

Lul - la - by, lul - la - by, lul - la -

61

66
pp
an - gels bright, Lul - la, lul - la - by, Guard thee till I come with light; Lul - la, lul - la-
an - gels bright, Lul - la, lul - la - by, Guard thee till I come with light;
pp
an - gels bright, Lul - la, lul - la - by, Guard thee till I come with light; Lul - la, lul - la-
pp
an - gels bright, Lul - la, lul - la - by, Guard thee till I come with light; Lul - la, lul - la-
pp
- by, Lul - la, lul - la - by, Guard thee till I come with light; Lul - la, lul - la-
66
72
- by, lul - la, lul - la - by, lul - la, lul - la - by.
pp
lul - la, lul - la - by, lul - la, lul - la - by, lul - la - by.
- by, O lul - la - by, lul - la - by, O lul - la - by, lul - la - by.
- by, O lul - la - by, lul - la - by, lul - la, lul - la - by.
div.
- by, lul - la - by, O lul - la - by, lul - la - by.
72

# 33. SOFTLY, SOFTLY, BLOW YE BREEZES

Text
Henry Kirk White

GEORGE ELVEY
(1816 - 1893)

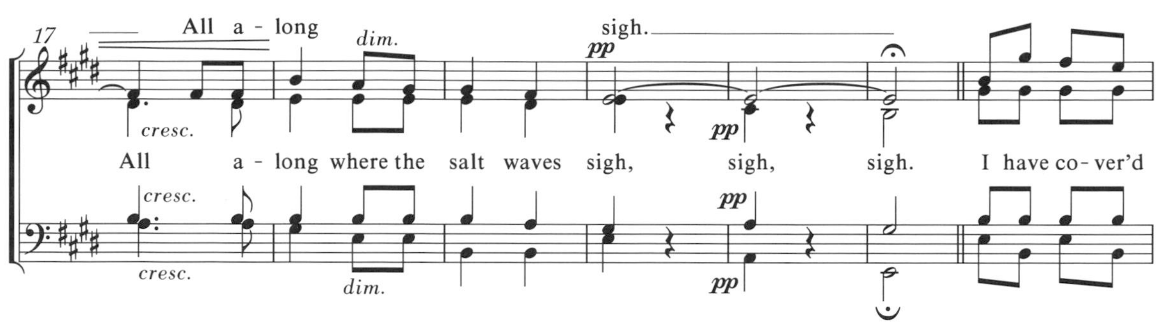
17
All a - long
dim.
sigh.
pp
cresc.
pp
All a - long where the salt waves sigh, sigh, sigh. I have co- ver'd
cresc.
pp
cresc.
dim.
pp

24
him with rush - es, Wa - ter flags and branch - es dry; Ed - wy, long have

28
been thy slum - bers, Ed - wy, Ed - wy, ope thine eyes. My love is a -

32
cresc.
dim.
sigh,
All a -
p
cresc.
cresc.
- sleep. He lies by the deep, All a - long where the salt waves sigh, All a -
cresc.
cresc.
dim.
p
cresc.

39
dim.
sigh
pp
- long where the salt waves sigh, sigh, sigh
Still he sleeps, he will_ not_ wak - en,
dim.
46
Fast - ly clo - sed_ is his eye; Pa - ler is his cheek and chil - ler,
50
cresc.
Than the i - cy moon on high. A - las! he is dead, He chose his death
cresc.
55
dim.
cresc.
sigh_ All a - long
bed, All a - long where the salt waves sigh All a - long where the
dim.
All_ a - long sigh._
61
salt waves sigh, All a - long where the salt waves sigh, sigh, sigh.
All a - long
where the salt_ waves

# 34. SONG OF PROSERPINE

Text
P.B. Shelley

SAMUEL COLERIDGE - TAYLOR
(1875 - 1912)

8 poco accel. largamente

div. unis. div.

bud and blos-som, Breathe thine in-fluence most di-vine On thine

bud and blos-som, Breathe thine in-fluence_ most_ di-vine On thine

div.

blade,_ bud and blos-som, Breathe thine in-fluence most_ di-vine On thine

div.

blade,_ bud and blos-som,_ Breathe_ thine_ in-fluence most di-vine On thine

8 poco accel. largamente

11 poco rit.

*ff* unis. *mf* *p*

own_ child,_ Pros-er-pine,_ Pros-er-pine._

*ff* unis. *mf* *p*

own_ child,_ Pros-er-pine,_ Pros-er-pine._

*ff* *mf* *p*

own_ child,_ Pros-er-pine,_ Pros-er-pine._

*ff* *mf* *p*

own child,_ Pros-er-pine,_ Pros-er-pine._

11 poco rit.

16
a tempo
div.
unis.
cresc.
If with mists of evening dew Thou dost nourish these young flowers
If with mists of evening dew Thou dost nourish these young flowers
If with mists of evening dew Thou dost nourish these young flowers
If with mists of evening dew Thou dost nourish these young flowers
16
a tempo
20
Till they grow in scent and hue Fair - est chil - - dren
Till they grow in scent and hue Fair - est chil - - dren
Till they grow in scent and hue Fair - est chil-dren, fair-est
Till they grow in scent and hue Fair - est chil-dren, fair-est
20

23

**poco accel.** **largamente**

div. unis. div.

of the Hours, Breathe thine in - fluence most di - vine On thine

div.

of the Hours, Breathe thine in - fluence_ most_ di - vine On thine

div.

chil- dren of the Hours, Breathe thine in - fluence most_ di - vine On thine

div.

chil - dren_ of the Hours,_ Breathe_ thine_ in - fluence most di - vine On thine

23

**poco accel.** **largamente**

26

**poco rall.**

unis. *ff* *mf* *p* *dim.* *ppp*

own_ child,_ Pros - er - pine,_ Pros - er - pine.

unis. *ff* *mf* *p* *dim.* *ppp*

own_ child,_ Pros - er - pine,_ Pros - er - pine.

*ff* *mf* *p* *dim.* *ppp*

own_ child,_ Pros - er - pine,_ Pros - er - pine.

*ff* *mf* *p* *dim.* *ppp*

own child,_ Pros - er - pine,_ Pros - er - pine.

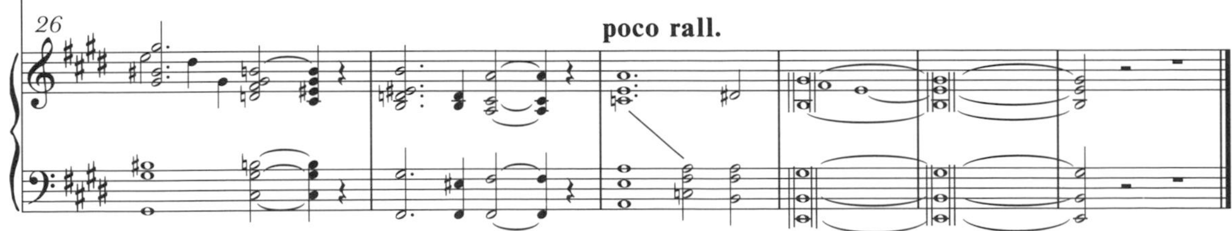

# 35. SWEET AND LOW

Text
Alfred, Lord Tennyson

JOSEPH BARNBY

# 36. SWEET CONTENT

Text
Thomas Dekker

JOHN JOUBERT
(b. 1927)

7
mf
Dost thou laugh to see how fools are vex'd To add to gold-en num-bers gold-en
mf
Dost thou laugh to see how fools are vex'd To add to gold-en num-bers
mf
Dost thou laugh to see how fools are vex'd To add to gold-en
mf
Dost thou laugh to see how fools are vex'd to add to
7
10
p
pp dolciss.
num - bers? O sweet con-tent! O sweet, O
p
pp dolciss.
gold-en num - bers? O sweet con-tent! O sweet, O
p
pp dolciss.
num-bers gold-en num - bers? O sweet con-tent! O sweet, O
p
pp dolciss.
gold-en num-bers gold-en num - bers? O sweet con-tent! O sweet, O
10

13
Allegro
p cresc. molto
sweet con - tent! O sweet con - tent! Work a - pace, work a - pace,
p cresc. molto
sweet con - tent! O sweet con - tent! Work a - pace, work a -
p cresc. molto
sweet con - tent! O sweet con - tent! Work a - pace, work a - pace,
f subito p
cresc. molto
sweet con - tent! Work a - pace, work a - pace,
13
Allegro
17
ff
work a - pace, a - pace, a - pace, a - pace, a - pace, a - pace;
ff
- pace, a - pace, a - pace, a - pace, a - pace, a - pace;
ff
work a - pace, a - pace, a - pace, a - pace, a - pace, a - pace;
ff
work a - pace, a - pace, a - pace, a - pace, a - pace a - pace;
17

21
poco meno mosso
p
Hon-est la-bour bears a love-ly face, Hon-est la-bour bears a love-ly
p
Hon - est la-bour bears a love-ly face, Hon - est la-bour bears a
p
Hon - est la-bour bears a love-ly face, Hon - est la-bour
p
Hon - est la-bour bears a love-ly face, Hon - est
21
poco meno mosso
26 
Allegro
p cresc. poco a poco
face; Then hey non-ny non-ny, hey non-ny
p cresc. poco a poco
love-ly face; Then hey, then
p cresc. poco a poco
bears a love-ly face; Then hey non-ny non-ny,
p cresc. poco a poco
la-bour bears a love-ly face; Then hey then
26
Allegro

31

*mf cresc.*

non-ny, then hey non-ny non-ny, hey non-ny

*mf cresc.*

hey, then hey, then

*mf cresc.*

hey non-ny non-ny, then hey non-ny non-ny,

*mf cresc.*

hey, then hey, then

31

35

*f cresc.*

non-ny, then hey non-ny non-ny non-ny non-ny non-ny non-ny non-ny

*f cresc.*

hey, then hey non-ny non-ny non-ny non-ny non-ny

*f cresc.*

hey non-ny non-ny, then hey non-ny non-ny non-ny non-ny

*f cresc.*

hey, then hey non-ny non-ny non-ny non-ny non-ny non-ny

35

39
ff
mf
non-ny non-ny non-ny non-ny non-ny non-ny non-ny
non-ny non-ny non-ny non-ny non-ny non-ny non-ny non-ny non-ny non-ny non-ny non-ny
non-ny non-ny non-ny non-ny non-ny non-ny non-ny non-ny non-ny non-ny non-ny non-ny
non-ny non-ny non-ny non-ny non-ny non-ny non-ny non-ny non-ny non-ny non-ny non-ny
43
p
mf
Tempo I
non-ny!
Canst drink the wa - ters of the
non-ny non-ny!
Canst drink the wa - ters of the
non-ny non-ny!
Canst drink the wa - ters of the
non-ny non-ny!
Canst drink the wa - ters of the
43
Tempo I

48
p
mf
crisp - èd spring? O sweet con - tent! Swim'st thou in wealth, yet sink'st in
crisp - èd spring? O sweet con - tent! Swim'st thou in wealth, yet sink'st in
crisp - èd spring? O sweet con - tent! Swim'st thou in wealth, yet sink'st in
crisp - èd spring? O sweet con - tent! Swim'st thou in wealth, yet sink'st in
48
51
ff
mf
thine own tears? O pun - ish - ment! Then he that pa - - tient - ly want's
thine own tears? O pun - ish - ment! Then he that pa - - tient - ly want's
thine own tears? O pun - ish - ment! Then he that pa -
thine own tears? O pun - ish - ment! Then he that pa -
51

54
cresc.
bur - den bears, No bur - - den bears but is a
cresc.
bur - - - - den bears, No bur - den bears but is a
cresc.
- tient - ly want's bur - den bears, No bur - - den
cresc.
- tient - ly want's bur - - - - den bears, No bur - den
54
56
ff
p subito
pp dolciss.
king, a king! O sweet con - tent! O sweet, O
king, a king! O sweet con-tent! O sweet, O
bears but is a king, a king! O sweet con- tent! O sweet, O
bears but is a king, a king! O sweet con- tent! O sweet, O
56

59

**Allegro**

*p cresc. molto*

sweet con - tent! O sweet con - tent! Work a - pace,

*p cresc. molto*

sweet con - tent! O sweet con - tent! Work a -

*p cresc. molto*

sweet con - tent! O sweet con - tent! Work a - pace,

*f subito* *p*

sweet con - tent! Work a - pace,

59

**Allegro**

62

work a - pace, work a - pace, a - pace,

- pace, work a - pace, a - pace, a -

work a - pace, work a - pace, a - pace,

*cresc. molto*

work a - pace, work a - pace, a - pace,

62

65

ff poco meno mosso p

— a-pace, a-pace, a-pace, a-pace; Hon-est la-bour bears a love-ly

-pace, a-pace, a-pace, a-pace, a-pace; Hon - est la-bour bears a

— a-pace, a-pace, a-pace, a-pace; Hon - est la-bour

— a-pace, a-pace, a-pace, a-pace; Hon - est

65

poco meno mosso

69

face, Hon-est la-bour bears a love-ly face; — Then

love-ly face, — Hon - est la-bour bears a love-ly face; —

bears a love-ly face, Hon - est la-bour bears a love-ly face; —

la-bour bears a love-ly face, — Hon - est la-bour bears a love-ly face; —

69

**Allegro**

74

*cresc. poco a poco*

hey non-ny non-ny, hey non-ny non-ny, *mf cresc.* then

*p cresc. poco a poco*

Then hey, then hey

*p cresc. poco a poco*

Then hey non-ny non-ny, hey non-ny

*p cresc. poco a poco*

Then hey, then hey,

74 **Allegro**

78

hey non-ny non-ny, hey non-ny non-ny, *f cresc.* then hey non-ny

*mf cresc.* then hey, then hey, *f cresc.* then hey

non-ny, *mf cresc.* then hey non-ny non-ny, hey non-ny non-ny, *f cresc.* then

*mf cresc.* then hey, then hey, *f cresc.* then hey

78

83
non-ny non-ny non-ny non-ny non-ny non-ny non-ny non-ny non-ny non-ny non-ny non-ny
non-ny non-ny non-ny non-ny non-ny non-ny non-ny non-ny non-ny non-ny
hey non-ny non-ny non-ny non-ny non-ny non-ny non-ny non-ny non-ny non-ny
non-ny non-ny non-ny non-ny non-ny non-ny non-ny non-ny non-ny non-ny non-ny non-ny
83
87
non-ny non-ny!
non-ny non-ny non-ny non-ny non-ny non-ny non-ny non-ny!
non-ny non-ny non-ny non-ny non-ny non-ny non-ny non-ny!
non-ny non-ny non-ny non-ny non-ny non-ny non-ny non-ny!
87

*To my friend Canon Gorton*

# 37. THERE IS SWEET MUSIC

Text
Alfred, Lord Tennyson

EDWARD ELGAR

* Some Altos should sing with the 1st Tenors.

6
ppp legato ed espress.
unis.
div.
There is sweet mu - sic
ppp legato ed espress.
div.
unis.
There is sweet mu - sic
unis.
div.
unis.
molto dim.
walls Of shad- owy gran - ite, in a gleam - ing pass;
unis.
molto dim.
walls Of shad- owy gran - ite, in a gleam - ing pass;
6
9
unis.
div.
unis.
div.
Mu -
p
here that soft - er falls Than pet - als from blown ro- ses on the grass;
div.
here that soft - er falls Than pet - als from blown ro- ses on the grass;
ppp
ppp
9

- - sic
12
mf ten.
p dim.
Mu - sic that gent - ler on the spi - rit lies,
p mf ten.
p
Mu - sic that gent - ler on the spi - rit lies,
Mu - sic
pp
unis.
Mu - sic that gent - lier on the
pp
Mu sic that gent - lier on the
12
14
ppp
pp
Than tir'd eye - lids up - on tir'd eyes;
That gent - lier lies, Than tir'd
pp
That gent - lier lies, Than tir'd
dim.
pp div. unis. ten.
spi - rit lies,
Mu - sic that gent - lier on the spi - rit lies,
dim.
unis. div. ten.
spi - rit lies,
Mu - sic that gent - lier on the spi - rit lies,
14

17
unis.
dim.
eye - - - lids up - on tir'd eyes;
div.
dim.
eye - - - lids up - on tir'd eyes;
Than tir'd eye - lids
p
div.
unis.
p dim.
up - on tir'd eyes;
Than tir'd eye - lids
p
dim.
unis.
p
up - on tir'd eyes,
up - on tir'd
17
18
mf
Mu - sic that brings sweet sleep,
Mu - - - sic
mf
Mu - sic that brings sweet sleep,
unis.
mf div. p cantabile
Mu - sic that brings sweet
sleep, that brings sweet sleep down from the
sleep, that brings sweet sleep down from the
div.
mf p cantabile
mf
eyes; Mu - sic that brings sweet sleep, that brings
18

20

p div.

that brings sweet sleep down from the bliss - - - ful skies.

p

that brings sweet sleep down from the bliss - - - ful skies.

bliss - - - ful sleep, that brings sweet sleep down from the

bliss - - - ful sleep, that brings sweet sleep down from the

sweet sleep, that brings sweet sleep down from the bliss - ful

20

22

mf unis. dim.

Here are cool moss-es deep, And in the stream the long-leaved

mf div. unis. div.

Here are cool moss-es deep, And thro' the moss the i-vies creep, And in the stream the

bliss - ful, bliss - - ful skies. Here are cool moss - es deep,

bliss - ful, bliss - - ful

skies, down from the bliss-ful skies, the bliss-ful skies.

22

25

poco rit.

ppp div. p unis.

flow - - ers weep, And from the crag-gy ledge the pop-py hangs in

unis. ppp p

flow - - ers weep, And from the crag-gy ledge the pop-py hangs in

pp

And in the stream the long-leaved flow - - ers weep,

And in the stream the long-leaved flow - - ers weep,

pp

The long-leaved flow - ers weep,

25

poco rit.

a tempo

28

pp pp ppp

sleep. Mu - sic that brings sweet sleep

pp pp ppp

sleep. Mu - sic that brings sweet sleep

pp unis. div.

and in the stream the long-leaved flow-ers weep, And from the crag-gy ledge the pop-py

pp unis.

and in the stream the long-leaved flow-ers weep, And from the crag-gy ledge the pop-py

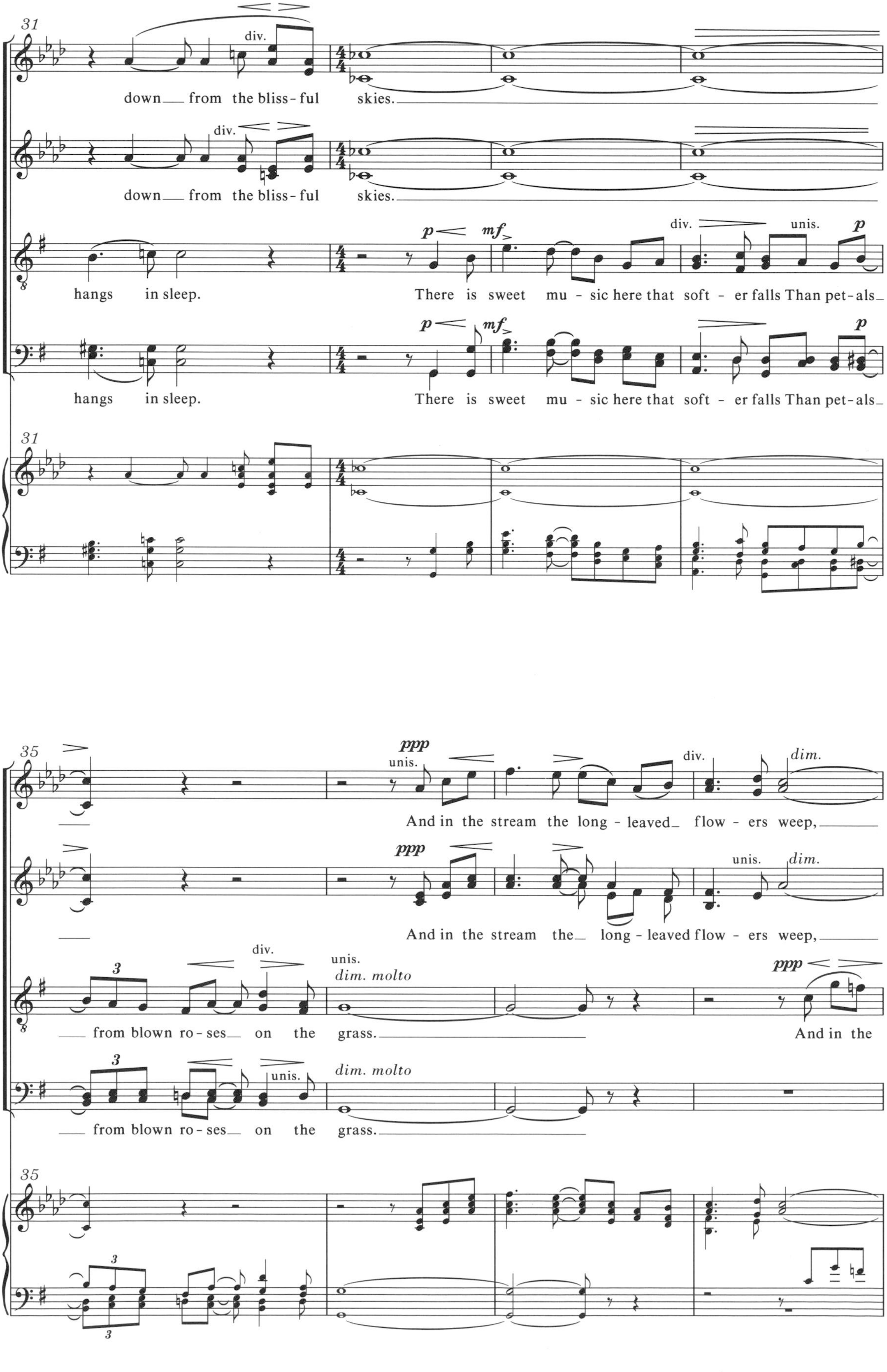
31
div.
down from the bliss - ful skies.
div.
down from the bliss - ful skies.
p mf div. unis. p
hangs in sleep. There is sweet mu - sic here that soft - er falls Than pet - als
p mf p
hangs in sleep. There is sweet mu - sic here that soft - er falls Than pet - als
31
35
ppp
unis. div. dim.
And in the stream the long - leaved flow - ers weep,
ppp unis. dim.
And in the stream the long - leaved flow - ers weep,
div. unis.
dim. molto
ppp
from blown ro - ses on the grass. And in the
unis.
dim. molto
from blown ro - ses on the grass.
35

39
poco
unis. dim.
And from the crag - gy ledge the pop-py hangs in sleep,
poco
div.
dim.
And from the crag - gy ledge the pop-py hangs in sleep,
And from the crag
div. pp
stream
And from the
pp
div.
pp
the flow-ers weep,
39
42
div.
dim.
rit. e dim.
pp
unis.
ppp
hangs in sleep, sleep, sleep, sleep, sleep.
dim.
pp
div.
ppp
hangs in sleep, sleep, sleep, sleep, sleep.
pp
ppp
pppp
pp
the pop-py hangs in sleep, sleep, sleep, sleep, sleep.
crag-gy ledge
unis.
div.
pp
ppp
pppp
pp
the pop-py hangs, the pop-py hangs in sleep, sleep, sleep, sleep.
42
rit. e dim.

# 38. THERE WAS AN OLD MAN IN A TREE

( No.3 of *Three Nonsense Songs* )

Text
Edward Lear

MÁTYÁS SEIBER
(1905 - 1965)

9
tree, Who was hor - ri - bly bored by a bee, by a bee, who was
tree, in a tree, a tree, in a tree, in a tree,
was an old man in a tree, Who was hor - ri - bly bored by a bee,
was an old man in a tree, a tree, a tree.
9
13
poco cresc.
hor - ri - bly, hor - ri - bly, hor - ri - bly, hor - ri - bly, hor - ri - bly bored by a bee
mf
hor - ri - bly, hor - ri - bly, hor - ri - bly, hor - ri - bly bored by a bee ee
hor - ri - bly, hor - ri - bly, hor - ri - bly bored by a bee ee
hor - ri - bly, hor - ri - bly bored by a bee ee
13

17
ee ee ee ee ee.
When they said,
ee ee ee ee ee ee.
When
ee ee ee ee ee ee.
When they said,
ee ee ee ee ee ee.
When they said,
17

22
when they said, when they said, when they said, when
they said, when they said, when they said, when they said, when
when they said, when they said, when they said, when they said,
when they said, when they said,
22

* Sing on *zz,* not on *u*.

36
spoken, matter of fact
f angry
-plied, 'Yes, it does! It's a re-gu-lar brute of a bee
spoken, matter of fact
f angry
-plied, 'Yes, it does! It's a re-gu-lar brute of a bee ee
spoken, matter of fact
f angry
-plied, 'Yes, it does! It's a re-gu-lar brute of a bee ee
spoken, matter of fact
f angry
-plied, 'Yes, it does! It's a re-gu-lar brute of a bee ee
36
40 
ee ee ee ee ee, It's a re-gu-lar brute of a bee!'
ff
ee ee ee ee ee ee, It's a re-gu-lar brute of a bee!'
ff
ee ee ee ee ee ee, It's a re-gu-lar brute of a bee!'
ff
ee ee ee ee ee ee, It's a re-gu-lar brute of a bee!'
ff
40

*To Mr. John Cook and Members of the Park Church Choral Society, Highbury*

# 39. TO DAFFODILS

Text
Robert Herrick

HAROLD DARKE
(1888 - 1976)

9
noon. Stay, stay, Un - til the hast - ing
noon. Stay, stay Un-til the hast-ing day Has run, stay un-
noon. Stay, stay, Un-til the hast-ing day Has run, stay, stay, un-
noon. Stay, stay, stay, Un-til the hast-ing
9
15
cresc. molto
rall.
molto rall.
Slower
day Has run But to the e-ven-song, And hav-ing pray'd to-
unis.
div.
-til the day has run But to the e-ven-song, And hav-ing pray'd to-
-til the day has run But to the e-ven-song, And hav-ing pray'd to-
day has run But to the e-ven-song, And hav-ing pray'd to-
15
rall.
molto rall.
Slower

21
molto rall.
Tempo I
pp
p
- ge- ther, We will go with you a- long. We have short time to stay, as you; We
- ge- ther, We will go with you a - long. We have short time to stay, as you; We
- ge- ther, We will go with you a- long. We have short time to stay, as you; We
div.
unis.
- ge- ther, We will go with you a- long. We have short time to stay, as you; We
26
f
molto
poco
have as short a Spring, As quick a growth to meet de- cay, As
have as short a Spring, as short a Spring, As quick a growth to meet de- cay, As
have as short a Spring, as short a Spring, As quick a growth to meet de- cay, As
have as short a Spring, as short a Spring, As quick a growth to meet de- cay, As

31

*cresc. molto* **rall.**

*f* *ff*

you, or a - ny-thing. We die, As your hours do, and dry A - - way,

*f* *cresc. molto* *ff* div.

you, or a - ny-thing. We die, As your hours do, and_ dry A-way,_ dry__ a - way,

*f* *cresc. molto* *ff*

you, or a - ny-thing. We die, As your hours_ do, and dry A-way, and_ dry a - way,__

*f* *cresc. molto* *ff* div.

you, or a - ny-thing. We die,__ As your hours do, and dry A - way,__

31

**rall.**

38

**molto rall.** **Slower** **molto rall.**

*pp* *ppp*

Like to the Sum-mer's rain, Or as the pearls of morn-ing dew,_ Ne'er_ to be found a-gain.

unis. *pp* *ppp*

Like to the Sum-mer's rain, Or as the pearls of morn-ing dew, Ne'er_ to be found a - gain.

*pp* *ppp*

Like to_ the Sum-mer's rain, Or as the pearls of morn-ing dew,_ Ne'er_ to be found a-gain.

unis. *pp* *ppp* div.

Like to the Sum-mer's rain, Or as the pearls of morn-ing dew, Ne'er to be found a-gain.

38

**molto rall.** **Slower** **molto rall.**

*For Mary*

# 40. TO MISS MARGERY WENTWORTH

(No.2 of *Three Portraits*)

Text
John Skelton

JOHN JOUBERT

8

Plain - ly I can - not glose; Ye be, as I di - vine, The

Plain - ly I can - not glose; Ye be, as I di - vine, The

Plain - ly I can - not glose; Ye be, as I di - vine, The

Plain - ly I can - not glose; Ye be, as I di - vine, The

8

12

pret - ty prim-rose, The good - - - - ly, good - - - - ly col - um-bine.

pret - ty prim-rose, The good - - - - ly, good - - - - ly col - um-bine.

pret - ty prim-rose, The good - - - - ly, good - - - - ly col - um-bine.

pret - ty prim-rose, The good - - - - ly, good - - - - ly col - - um -

12

16
p
Be-nign, cour-teous, and meek, With
div. p
Be-nign, cour-teous, and meek,
p
Be-nign, cour-teous, and meek, With
div. p
- bine.
Be-nign, cour-teous, and meek,
16
21
word-es well de-vised;
mf
In
mf
With word-es well de-vised;
word-es well de-vised;
mf
In
mf
With word-es well de-vised;
21

25
f
you, who list to seek, Be
mf
f
In you, who list to seek, Be
f
you, who list to seek, Be
mf
f
In you, who list to seek, Be
25
29
mf
p
vir - tues well com - prised, be vir - tues well com - prised, be
mf
p
vir - tues well com - prised, be vir - tues well com - prised, be
mf
p
vir - tues well com - prised, be vir - tues well com - prised, be
mf
p
vir - tues well com - prised, be vir - tues well com - prised, be
29

33
vir - tues well com - prised.
unis.
vir - - tues, be vir - tues well com - prised.
vir - tues well com - prised, be vir - tues well com -
vir - - tues well com - -
33
36
poco rall.
a tempo
pp
With mar - ger-ain gen - tle, The flower of good - li - head,
With mar - ger-ain gen - tle, The flower of good - li - head,
- prised. With mar - ger-ain gen - tle, The flower of good - li - head,
unis.
- prised. With mar - ger-ain gen - tle, The flower of good - li - head,
36
poco rall.
a tempo

39
Em - broid - ered the man - tle Is of your maid - en - head.
Em - broid - ered the man - tle Is of your maid - en - head.
Em - broid - ered the man - tle Is of your maid - en - head.
Em - broid - ered the man - tle Is of your maid - en - head.
39
42
Plain - ly I can - not glose; Ye be, as I di -
Plain - ly I can - not glose; Ye be, as I di -
Plain - ly I can - not glose; Ye be, as I di -
Plain - ly I can - not glose; Ye be, as I di -
42

46
vine, The pret - ty prim - rose, The good - - - - - - ly,
vine, The pret - ty prim - rose, The good - - - - - - ly,
vine, The pret - ty prim - rose, The good - - - - - - ly,
vine, The pret - ty prim - rose, The good - - - - - - ly,
46
49
good - - - - - - ly col - - - - - - - um - bine.
good - - - - - - ly col - - - - - - - um - bine.
good - - - - - - ly col - - - - - - - um - bine.
div.
good - - - - - - ly col - - - - - - - um - bine.
49

*Composed for the Bristol Madrigal Society*

# 41. TUNE THY MUSIC TO THY HEART

Text
Thomas Campion

HENRY WALFORD DAVIES
(1869-1941)

* This should be sung by a solo voice provided it can be made to blend perfectly with the chorus trebles; but in any case the 'fa la las' and the last page should be sung by all.

21
thanks and so thy sor - row: Though De - vo - tion needs not
joy, and so thy sor - row: Though De - vo - tion needs
joy, and so thy sor - - row: Though De - vo - tion
thanks and so thy sor - row: Though De - vo - tion needs not
joy, and so thy sor - row: Though De - vo - tion
28
art, Some - - time of the poor the rich may bor - row.
not art, Some - time of the poor the rich may bor - row.
needs not art, Some - time of the poor the rich may bor - row.
art, Some - - time of the poor the rich may bor - row.
needs not art, Some - time of the poor the rich may bor - row.

34
pp
Fa la la la la la la la la la la la, Fa la la la la,
pp
Fa la la la la la la la la la la,  Fa la
pp
Fa la la la la la la la, Ah!
pp
Fa la la la la la la la la,  Fa
pp
Fa la la la la la, Fa la la la
34
37
p
Fa la la la la la, Ah! Fa la la.
p
la, Fa la la la la la la, Ah! Fa la la,
p
Fa la la la la, Ah! Ah! Fa la la,
p
la la la la la la, Ah! Ah! Fa la la la
p
la, Fa la la la la, Ah! Ah! Fa la la,
37

* See footnote on page 227

55
out - ward praise, On - - ly strives to shew a love un -
- fects not praise, On - - ly strives to shew a love un -
- fects not praise, On - - ly strives to shew a love un -
out - ward praise, On - - ly strives to shew a love un -
- fects not out-ward praise On - ly strives to shew a love un -
55
61
mf
- feign - ed. Fa la la la la, shew a
p
mf
- feign - ed. Fa la la la la, Fa la la la la, shew a love, a
p
mf
- feign - ed. Fa la la la la, Fa la la la la la la la, shew a
mf
- feign - ed. shew a
p
mf
- feign - ed. Fa la la la la, Fa la la la la, Fa la la la la,
61

* See footnote on page 227

79
molto tranquillo
pp
(ten.)
(ppp)
Love the High - est doth res - pect; Love a - lone to Him
Love the High - est doth res - pect; Love a - lone to Him
Love the High - est doth res - pect; Love a - lone to Him
div.
Love the High - est doth res - pect; Love a - lone to Him
div.
Love the High - est doth res - pect; Love a - lone to Him
79
molto tranquillo
79
is ev - er pleas - ing, ev - er pleas - ing.
is ev - er pleas - ing, ev - er pleas - ing.
is ev - er pleas - ing, ev - er pleas - ing.
unis.
is ev - er pleas - ing, ev - er pleas - ing.
unis.
div.
unis.
is ev - er pleas - ing, ev - er pleas - ing.
79

# 42. UNDER THE GREENWOOD TREE

( No.2 of *Three Choral Songs from 'As You Like It'* )

Text
William Shakespeare

JOSEPH HOROVITZ
(b. 1926)

𝅗𝅥 = 69 (equal crotchets throughout)
SOPRANO
ALTO
TENOR
BASS
Un - der the green - wood tree Who loves to lie with me, And
tune his mer - ry note Un - to the sweet bird's throat, _
Come hith - er, come hith - er, come hith - er, come hith - er, come hith - er: ___ Here
div.
unis.
shall he see No en - e - my ___ But win - ter, but win - ter, but

17
f
win - ter and rough weath - er. Here shall he see No en - e - my But
f

21
1
win - ter, but win - ter, but win - ter and rough weath - er.

26
p
Who doth am - bi - tion shun, And loves to live i' the sun, Seek - ing the food he
p
div.
unis.
3

31
mf
p
2
p
ff
div.
eats, And pleas'd with what he gets, rough weath - er.
mf
p
p
ff
div.

# 43. WEEP YOU NO MORE

8
mf
snow - y moun - tains Heavn's Sun doth gent - ly
[mf]
- - - - - - - y moun-tains Heavn's Sun doth gent - ly
[mf]
how the snow-y moun-tains Heavn's Sun doth
[mf]
Look how the snow - y moun - tains Heavn's Sun
8
11 [mp]
[p]
waste. But my Sun's heav'n - ly eyes view not your
[mp]
[p]
waste. But my Sun's heav'n - ly eyes view not your
[mp]
[p]
waste. But my Sun's heav'n - ly eyes view not your
[mp]
[p]
doth gent-ly waste. But my Sun's heav'n - ly eyes view not your
11

14
[mf]
[mp]
weep-ing, That now lies sleep - - - - ing Soft - ly, soft - ly,
[mf] [mp]
weep-ing, That now lies sleep - - - - ing Soft - ly, soft - ly,
[mf]
[mp]
weep-ing,s That now lies sleep - ing Soft - - ly, now
[mf] [mp]
weep - - - - - ing, That now lies sleep - ing Soft-ly, now soft - ly,
14
17
[p]
[pp]
[p]
soft - ly, lies Sleep-ing, sleep-ing. Sleep is
[p] [pp] [p]
soft - ly lies Sleep-ing, sleep-ing. Sleep is a
[p] [pp] [p]
soft - ly lies Sleep-ing, sleep-ing. Sleep is a
[p] [pp] [p]
soft - ly lies Sleep-ing, sleep-ing. Sleep
17

22
a re-con-cil-ing, A rest that peace be-
re-con-cil-ing, A rest that peace be-
re-con-cil-ing, A rest that peace be-
is a re-con-cil-ing, A rest that peace be-
22
25
[mf]
[dim.]
-gets. Doth not the sun-rise smil-ing When
-gets. Doth not the sun-rise smil-ing When
-gets. Doth not the sun-rise sun-rise smil-ing
-gets. Doth not the sun-rise smil-ing when
25

28
[p]
[mp cresc.]
fair at ev'n he sets?
Rest you then,
[dim.]
fair at ev'n he sets?
Rest you then,
When fair at ev'n he sets?
When fair at ev'n he sets?
31
[f]
[mf]
rest, sad eyes, Melt not in weep - - - - - - ing
rest, sad eyes,
Melt not in
rest, sad eyes,
rest, sad eyes, Melt not in weep - - - - - - ing

34
[mf]
[dim.]
[f]
[mp]
While she lies Soft - - - ly, soft - ly, now
weep - - - - - - - - - - - - - ing While she lies
While she lies
While she lies
37
[p]
[pp]
[ppp]
soft - ly lies Sleep - ing, soft - - - ly sleep - ing.
soft - ly soft - ly, Sleep - ing, soft - - - ly sleep - ing.
soft - ly soft - ly, Sleep - ing, soft - - - ly sleep - ing.
soft - ly soft - ly, Sleep - ing, soft - - - ly sleep - ing.

# 44. WHICH IS THE PROPEREST DAY TO SING

THOMAS ARNE
(1710-78)

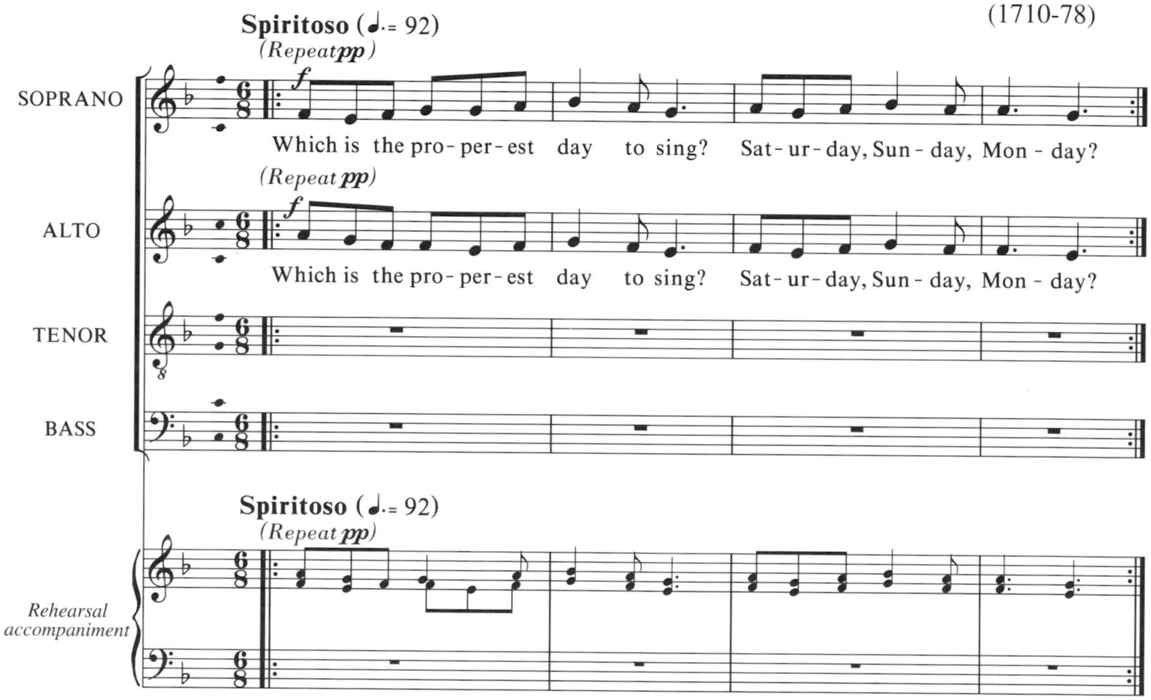

**Spiritoso** (♩. = 92)
*(Repeat* ***pp****)*

SOPRANO: Which is the pro- per- est day to sing? Sat- ur- day, Sun - day, Mon - day?

ALTO: Which is the pro- per- est day to sing? Sat- ur- day, Sun - day, Mon - day?

TENOR

BASS

**Spiritoso** (♩. = 92)
*(Repeat* ***pp****)*

*Rehearsal accompaniment*

9
f
Tell me but yours, I'll men - tion my day, Let us but fix on some day,
f
Tell me but yours, I'll men - tion my day, Let us but fix on some day,
f
Why, why should I name but one day,
f
Why, why should I name but one day?
9
13
p
Tell me but yours, I'll men - tion my day, Let us but fix on some day,
p
f
Tell me but yours, I'll men - tion my day, Let us but fix on some day,
p
f
Why, why, why should I name but one day?
p
f
Why, why, why should I name but one day?
13

17
p
f
Which? which? Let us but fix on some day.
Which? which? Let us but fix on some day. Bra - vo!
Each to be sure, 'tis a might - y fine thing! Why should I name but one day? Tues - day, Wednes - day,
Each to be sure, 'tis a might - y fine thing! Why should I name but one day? Tues - day, Wednes - day,
17
22
Bra - vo, bra - vo! Tues - day, Wednes - day, Thurs - day, Fri - day,
bra - vo! Why should I name but one day? Tues - day, Wednes - day, Thurs - day, Fri - day,
Thurs - day, Fri - day, Sat - ur - day, Sun - day, Mon - day, Tues - day, Wednes - day, Thurs - day, Fri - day,
Thurs - day, Fri - day, Sat - ur - day, Sun - day, Mon - day, Tues - day, Wednes - day, Thurs - day, Fri - day,
22

Published by Novello Publishing
Music setting by Stave Origination

Printed and bound in Great Britain by
Caligraving Limited Thetford Norfolk

6789